Nine Mile
Magazine

Vol 6, No. 1
Fall, 2018

NINE MILE MAGAZINE
Vol 6, No. 1 Fall, 2018

Publisher: Nine Mile Art Corp.
Editors: Bob Herz, Stephen Kuusisto, Andrea Scarpino
Art Editor Emeritus: Whitney Daniels
Cover Art: "Crossword," by Thomasina deMaio, 10 inches by 12 inches,
oil on canvas 2016

The publishers gratefully acknowledge support of the New York State
Council on the Arts with the support of Governor Andrew M. Cuomo
and the New York State Legislature. We also acknowledge support of
the County of Onondaga and CNY Arts through the Tier Three Project
Support Grant Program. We have also received significant support
from the Central New York Community Foundation. This publication
would not have been possible without the generous support of these
groups. We are very grateful to them all.

ISBN-10: 1-7326600-1-8
ISBN-13: 978-1-7326600-1-4

The poems of Sam Hamill included here are reprinted from *Habitation
Collected Poems*, by permission of the publisher, Lost Horse Press, to
which we register our gratitude.

Contents

About Nine Mile Magazine

Nine Mile Magazine publishes twice yearly, showcasing the best work we receive from authors whose work, energy, and vision are deeply entangled with life.

We at *Nine Mile Magazine* are committed to featuring diverse writers, including writers with mental and physical disabilities, and writers from different races, genders, ages, sexual identities, cultures, and religions.

SUBMISSIONS

For consideration in the magazine, submit 4 - 6 poems in Word or text at editor@ninemile.org. You can access a submission form at our website, ninemile.org. Please include:

- your name and contact information (email and home address for sending contributor's copies)
- a paragraph about yourself (background, achievements, etc),
- a statement of your aesthetic intent in the work ,
- a photo of yourself

We respond within 2 weeks. If you do not hear from us, reconnect to make sure we received your submission. Note that we do not accept unsolicited essays, reviews, video / motion based art, or Q&A's.

TALK ABOUT POETRY PODCASTS AND BLOG

At our Talk About Poetry podcast working poets discuss poems that interest, annoy, excite, and engage them. The Talk About Poetry blog provides more opportunities for feedback. The addresses are:

- *Soundcloud*: https://soundcloud.com/bobherz;
- *iTunes*: https://itunes.apple.com/us/podcast/talk-about-poetry/id972411979?mt=2;
- *Talk About Poetry blog*: https://talkaboutpoetry.wordpress.com

NINE MILE BOOKS

Nine Mile Books are available through our website, ninemile.org, or online at Amazon.com. Our most recent books are:

- *A Little Gut Magic*, Matthew Lippman (2018), $16. "Reading Matthew Lippman's poems feels like having a conversation with a hilarious, brutally honest, and brilliant friend."—Jessica Bacal, author of *Mistakes I Made at Work: 25 Influential Women Reflect on What They Got Out of Getting It Wrong.*

- *The Golem Verses*, Diane Wiener (2018), $16, or $9.99 at Kindle and iBooks. Of this book the poet Georgia Popoff has written, "…Diane Wiener unlocks the door to a room of confidences, secrets, passions, and fears. These poems present an interior dialogue in which the Golem is more than symbol or legend but trusted companion and guiding, grounding force. This room is furnished with intellect, wonder, inquiry, discovery, revelation, and release. Curl up in a comfy chair and bear witness to this lyric journey."

- *Perfect Crime*, David Weiss (2017), $16. Of this book the poet says, "The whole of it thinks about the idea of perfect crime metaphysically, in the sense that time, for example, is, itself, a perfect crime. Perfect meaning: effect without cause. A crime or situation or condition that can't be solved."

- *Where I Come From* (2016), Jackie Warren-Moore, $12. Poet, playwright, theatrical director, teacher, and freelance writer, Ms. Warren-Moore's work has been published nationally and internationally. She is a Survivor, of racism, sexism, sexual abuse, and physical abuse, who regards her poetic voice as the roadmap of her survival, a way of healing herself and of speaking to the souls of others.

- *Selected Late Poems of Georg Trakl* (2016), translations by Bob Herz, $7.50 plus mailing, or $7.49 at Kindle and iBooks. This book includes all the poems Trakl wrote in the last two years of his life, from *Sebastian in Dream* and the poems that appeared in *Der Brenner*, plus some poems from other periods showing the development of the poet's art.

- *Letter to Kerouac in Heaven* (2016) by Jack Micheline, $10. One of the original Beats, Michelin's career took him from Greenwich Village to San Francisco, with friends that included almost everyone, from Mailer to Ginsberg to Corso and others. He was a street poet whose first book included an introduction by Jack Kerouac and was reviewed in *Esquire* by Dorothy Parker. This is a replica publication of one of his street books.

- *Bad Angels*, Sam Pereira (2015). $20; or on Kindle and iBooks, $9.99. Of this poet Peter Everwine wrote, "He's an original." Pereira's work has been praised by Norman Dubie, David St. John, and Peter Campion.

- *Some Time in the Winter*, Michael Burkard (2014). $16. A reprint of the famed original 1978 chapbook with an extended essay by Mr. Burkard on the origins of the poem.

- *Poems for Lorca*, Walt Shepperd (2012). $9.95. The poems continue Mr. Shepperd's lifelong effort to truly see and record the life around him. Lorca is his daughter, and the poems constitute an invaluable generational gift from father to daughter, and from friend, colleague, and community member to all of us.

Nine Mile Magazine

Vol 6, No. 1
Fall, 2018

Appreciations & Asides

Miscellaneous notes gathered from here and there on art, literature, and life, from artists and critics we love or statements we find curiously interesting.

■ FOR THE SAKE OF A FEW LINES ONE MUST SEE MANY cities, men and things. One must know the animals, one must feel how the birds fly and know the gesture with which the small flowers open in the morning. One must be able to think back to roads in unknown regions, to unexpected meetings and to partings which one had long seen coming; to days of childhood that are still unexplained, to parents that one had to hurt when they brought one some joy and one did not grasp it (it was joy for someone else); to childhood illness that so strangely began with a number of profound and grave transformations, to days in rooms withdrawn and quiet and to mornings by the sea, to the sea itself, to seas, to nights of travel that rushed along on high and flew with all the stars-and it is not enough if one may think all of this. One must have memories of many nights of love, none of which was like the others, of the screams of women in labor, and of light, white, sleeping women in childbed, closing again. But one must also have been beside the dying, one must have sat beside the dead in the room with the open window and the fitful noises. And still it is not enough to have memories. One must be able to forget them when they are many, and one must have the great patience to wait until they come again. For it is not yet the memories themselves. Not until they have turned to blood within us, to glance, to gesture, nameless and no longer to be distinguished from ourselves-not until then can it happen that in a most rare hour the first word of a verse arises in their midst and goes forth from them..
—Rainer Maria Rilke, *The Notebooks of Malte Laurids Brigge* (original 1910; Dalkey Archive Press; New Translation edition, October 1, 2008)

■ POETIC TONE IS MORE THAN THE SPEAKING VOICE in which the poem happens; much more. Its roots go deep into the history and sociology of the craft. Even today, for a poet, tone is not a matter of the aesthetic of any one poem. It grows more surely, and more

painfully, from the ethics of the art. Its origins must always be in a suffered world rather than a conscious craft.
—Eavan Boland, A review of Elizabeth Bishop, "Time, Memory and Obsession," *PN Review*, Vol. 18, No. 2,

■ IF YOUR NEXT BIRTHDAY WILL BE YOUR EIGHTIETH, and you have read the greatest poetry all your life, then you begin to know that in the face of dying and death, the imagination is at once nothing and everything. Hamlet, the Western imagination incarnate, knows he is nothing and everything in himself, yet he is poetry itself, the center of the single, most unbelievably capacious consciousness that ever has imbued a body of literature. The Bible, Homer, Dante, Cervantes, Tolstoy, and Proust do not fade into the light of Shakespeare's dawn, but they edge toward reflecting a sun at the heart of reality. My assertion merely attempts to describe a generic experience of readership. All of Shakespeare together forms the Last Poem upon which we rely even as we forget the terms of our dependence.
—Bloom, Harold. *Till I End My Song: A Gathering of Last Poems* (HarperCollins, 2011)

■ NOTICE HOW FREQUENTLY THE CONCLUDING couplets of the sonnets are poor. Unlike many of even the greatest artists, Shakespeare is not interested in completely flawless wholes. He says what he wants to say and lets the sonnet end anyhow. But that is the fault of a major artist, for a minor one always completes the work carefully. For instance, when we read Dostoevsky, we feel, yes, this is wonderful, this is marvelous, now go home and write it all over again. And yet if he did, the effect might well be lost.
—W.H. Auden, *Lectures on Shakespeare* (Princeton University Press, 2000)

■YOU CAN ONLY WRITE REGULARLY IF YOU'RE WILLING to write badly. You can't write regularly and well. One should accept bad writing as a way of priming the pump, a warm-up exercise that allows you to write well.
—Jennifer Egan, *Why We Write: 20 Acclaimed Authors on How and Why They Do What They Do* (Plume, 2013)

■ RILKE HAS FOR HUNDREDS OF READERS BEEN THEIR first introduction to poetry that goes steeply and unapologetically up with the spirit. One could say that when a young man or woman encounters him, he will slip his hand under the elbow and guide the person on to some small house that stands nearby, perhaps a hut where the railway switchman lives. Once inside, the young person notices that the ceiling is higher than one would have thought. In fact, the hut is a cathedral, with immensely high vaults, like Chartres, with deep shadows. Meanwhile, Rilke pretends that nothing unusual has happened.
—Robert Bly, *The Winged Energy of Delight* (HarperCollins, 2004)

■THE TASTE OF THE APPLE (STATES BERKELEY) LIES in the contact of the fruit with the palate, not in the fruit itself; in a similar way (I would say) poetry lies in the meeting of poem and reader, not in the lines of symbols printed on pages of a book. What is essential is... the thrill, the almost physical emotion that comes with each reading.
—Jorge Luis Borges, *Selected Poems 1923–1967*, edited, with an Introduction and Notes, by Norman Thomas Giovanni (Dell, New York, 1973)

■ WHEN I AM WORKING ON A BOOK OR A STORY I WRITE every morning as soon after first light as possible. There is no one to disturb you and it is cool or cold and you come to your work and warm as you write. You read what you have written and, as you always stop when you know what is going to happen next, you go on from there. You write until you come to a place where you still have your juice and know what will happen next and you stop and try to live through until the next day when you hit it again. You have started at six in the morning, say, and may go on until noon or be through before that. When you stop you are as empty, and at the same time never empty but filling, as when you have made love to someone you love. Nothing can hurt you, nothing can happen, nothing means anything until the next day when you do it again. It is the wait until the next day that is hard to get through.
—Ernest Hemingway, "The Art of Fiction No. 21," *Paris Review*, Issue 18, Spring 1958.

■ AN ORIENTAL WISE MAN ALWAYS USED TO ASK THE divinity in his prayers to be so kind as to spare him from living in an interesting era. As we are not wise, the divinity has not spared us and we are living in an interesting era. In any case, our era forces us to take an interest in it. The writers of today know this. If they speak up, they are criticized and attacked. If they become modest and keep silent, they are vociferously blamed for their silence. In the midst of such din the writer cannot hope to remain aloof in order to pursue the reflections and images that are dear to him. Until the present moment, remaining aloof has always been possible in history. When someone did not approve, he could always keep silent or talk of something else. Today everything is changed and even silence has dangerous implications. The moment that abstaining from choice is itself looked upon as a choice and punished or praised as such, the artist is willy-nilly impressed into service. "Impressed" seems to me a more accurate term in this connection than "committed." Instead of signing up, indeed, for voluntary service, the artist does his compulsory service.

—Albert Camus, "Create Dangerously," *Resistance, Rebellion, and Death: Essays* (Vintage; Reissue edition, 1995)

■A POET IS SOMEBODY WHO FEELS, AND WHO expresses his feelings through words.

This may sound easy. It isn't.

A lot of people think or believe or know they feel — but that's thinking or believing or knowing; not feeling. And poetry is feeling — not knowing or believing or thinking.

Almost anybody can learn to think or believe or know, but not a single human being can be taught to feel. Why? Because whenever you think or you believe or you know, you're a lot of other people: but the moment you feel, you're nobody-but-yourself.

To be nobody-but-yourself — in a world which is doing its best, night and day, to make you everybody else — means to fight the hardest battle which any human being can fight; and never stop fighting.

—E.E. Cummings, *E.E. Cummings: A Miscellany Revised* (October House, 1965)

■I BEGAN TRANSLATING WITH THE IDEA THAT IT COULD teach me something about writing poetry. The great exemplar, of course, was Pound. The neo-Flaubertian image of poetry as a "craft" was in all the ikons I could see. Unfortunately something of the "how" of writing poetry is probably always important, a reminder of the ambivalences of our imperfection and our artifice. And every way of learning it, and the learning itself as it is acquired, has peculiar dangers. Translation may be no more dangerous than any other to a growing recognition of the true original that, in del Vasto's words, "tastes of the source." It is love, I imagine, more than learning, that may eventually make it possible to be aware of the living resonance before it has words, to keep the distinction clear between mere habit and the style that is some part, at least, of the man, and will impel one to be wary of any skill coming to shadow and doctor the source, any deftness usurping the authority it was reared to serve. "When I pronounce men to be quick of hearing," Chuang Tzu wrote, "I do not mean that they hearken to anything else, but that they hearken to themselves." Which of course, is the true and exacting vocation of the poet's ear, a matter of origin before it is one of learning. But every time the words are found, the finding is a contribution to learning as well, and it may be in the interest of clarity if some of the learning is obviously distinct from the particular source in oneself.
—W.S. Merwin, *Selected Translations* (Copper Canyon Press, 2013)

■ IT'S NOT ALWAYS EASY TO TELL THE DIFFERENCE between thinking and looking out of the window.
—Wallace Stevens, *Letters* (1966)

■ THE FIRST MISTAKE OF ART IS TO ASSUME THAT IT'S serious. I could even be an asshole here and say that "Nothing is true; everything is permitted," which is true as a matter of fact, but people might get the wrong idea. What's truest is that you cannot enslave a fool.
—Lester Bangs, "James Taylor Marked for Death."

In Praise of Sam Hamill

A Remembrance of Sam Hamill

Everyone it seemed knew a piece of Sam Hamill—as poet, as editor, as translator, as friend, as activist, as irascible figure who occupied some felt and important place in our lives. A gargantuanly active figure on many fronts, he was most of all a brilliant editor and publisher who made Copper Canyon into a powerhouse publishing company that changed the face of poetry in America, bringing in voices from other countries and resurrecting poets who would have been neglected and back-listed but for his efforts.

Adopted from foster care at age three, Hamill had experiences with violence and theft, and did some jail time as result. He said that his adoptive parents were abusive, and that as a teenager he ran away from home, making it to San Francisco, where he began using heroin. Despite this unpromising background, he became somehow interested in poetry, and during a judge-ordained enlistment in the Marine Corps, he read Camus's essays on pacifism and discovered Zen literature. "Poetry gave me a reason for being," he later said. "And I'm not exaggerating when I say that. My ethics, my sense of morality, my work ethic, my sense of compassion for suffering humanity, all of that comes directly out of the practice of poetry."

He attended Los Angeles Valley College and the University of California, Santa Barbara, where he studied with Kenneth Rexroth. He won a $500 award for producing the best university literary magazine in the country, and with that money cofounded the all-poetry Copper Canyon Press in Denver, Colorado. Copper Canyon later joined with the nonprofit arts organization Centrum in Port Townsend, Washington. Hamill was editor-printer for the press from 1972 to 2004. Its list expanded to over 400 titles and included collections by both older and emerging American poets, translations, re-issues of out-of-print poetry classics, prose about poetry, and anthologies. It was an important and necessary performance that contributed to the vitality of poetry in this country.

Hamill wanted to change the world through poetry, and his moral sensibility and need to act led him inevitably into political activism. In 2003, he organized Poets Against the War after first lady Laura Bush invited him to a poetry symposium at the White House. Rather than simply decline the invitation as a way of expressing his opposition to what was then the impending Iraq invasion, he solicited anti-war verse from poets around the country and planned to present them at the symposium. The White House postponed the event. Hamill created poetsagainstthewar.org, an online anthology that collected over 20,000 poems of protest and spawned an international movement. He later edited a collection from the website, *Poets Against the War* (2003). As he said in a 2006 interview, "You can't write about character and the human condition and be apolitical—that's not the kind of world we've ever lived in."

In addition to all this activity, Sam was a terrific poet, and his work has been collected in *Habitation: Collected Poems* (2014, Lost Horse Press), to which we express our gratitude for allowing the reprint of so many poems here. His final book is *After Morning Rain* (Tiger Bark Press, 2018), reviewed here. We also present an interview with Sam, by our editor Andrea Scarpino, in which Sam's candidness is on full display. *Publisher's Weekly* said of his poetry that it "presents a model of honest, consistent, undisguised political engagement: he articulates not only a vision of peace with justice, not only his relish for work to achieve that vision, but his sense of the role that poetry can play." Influences show in the work—Ezra Pound, Kenneth Rexroth, Denise Levertov, Hayden Carruth—but the poems are finally Sam's. As Steve Kuusisto says is his piece on Hamill, "I place Hamill alongside Denise Levertov, Adrienne Rich, Rexroth, and Snyder because they are collectively steeped in the 'real work' of overcoming apprehension, disquiet and restlessness." Kuusisto in the essay rightly praises Hamill's maturity.

Hamill was awarded fellowships from the National Endowment for the Arts, the Guggenheim Foundation, the Woodrow Wilson Foundation, and the Mellon Fund, and he won the Stanley Lindberg Lifetime Achievement Award for Editing and the Washington Poets Association Lifetime Achievement Award. He died in 2018 at age 74 of chronic obstructive pulmonary disease.

He left behind an extraordinary body of work, some of which we are pleased to be able to share and celebrate here.

Sam Hamill

Dead Letter (II)

To love the dead is easy. —William Matthews

Father, it is May again,
and I enter the thirty-seventh year
of my search. I have walked again
the long path through the woods
when ocean spray and ferns,
blackberry shoots and
the blossoming apple
wear the jewels of fine mist
into the afternoon. The juncos
this morning burst into song
shortly after four. I lay in bed
and listened. I remembered
the heavy silence of the Salt Flats
as we crossed them in the heat
of 1948, the sulfurous white teeth
of Kali grinning all the way
to Reno. If there are gods
of the desert lands, they are women
and angry and just. I have seen
in the heart of the Escalante
just enough life for hope:
hope for respite, for a better
life to come, or hope
to end a life of pain.

I watch the starlings chase
ravens down endless ravines
of sky. Far below them,
the logged-off stubble and slash
of minds gone wild and narrow,
and I remember my grandfather,

Otto Empey, and I think
of what he never said, and of
the Taylors down in Moab, Lester's
great hands on the pommel
of his saddle astride
his buckskin mare. It is good work
that leaves us in the weather,
in the rains that fall
on all of us, living and dead
alike, in the blank snows
of memory that cool our dreams
and fill our lives with stillness.

And I can hear, coming
over hills of woods, the soft breath
of the sea. Here, in the country
of Chemekum and Makah,
where rich robes warmed them
in winter, robes of cedar bark
and otter, where they brought down
their animals with stones
for maybe fifteen thousand years—
I am home. In the gray light
of early afternoon,
I can smell thistle and salmon
and the smoke of an alder fire
drifting over the dreamscape
of women and men and babies—
all who went before. I can hear
their chanting from far off,
from across the edge of the sea,
and see, perhaps, their longboats
slide across a bay. It is easy
to love the dead for what
they did or what they didn't say.

When I gaze out far enough,
I can see where the sea meets
the sky—the dark approaches
that promise to return.
And as I turn toward my life
once more, it is the daily
I adore: the little pleasure,
the food and drink of necessity.
Down on Water Street, among
the fruit flies and oranges
and lemons, apples, and tangerines,
I'll pick among the artichokes
for one ripe and green, just right,
and boil it in water, and eat
the fleshy pulp of its leaves
scraped from around the thorns,
eat down into the soft green heart,
and remember you then who taught
me how, and then slightly bow
with neither praise nor blame,
and from my knees in the dusk
I'll pray once more for nothing,
for the dead,
and for the gifts they bring.

Friend

It's barely October, but almost
overnight, it's autumn.

A few lank strands of sunlight
dangle through the clouds.

The hawks stopped circling meadows
and moved toward trees where varmints nest

building secret places for the winter.
The days grow fainter, and the shadows last forever

I would like to sit outside today,
to drag my rocker out to the deck and sit

and listen to your stories.
I would like to sit outside in my rocker

and pour you a glass of bourbon.
See, back in that corner,

in the shadows of the cedar,
you see that Japanese maple?

It turned yellow and red last Tuesday.
Monday it was vermillion.

I love that goddamn tree. Autumn here
is otherwise so subtle.

But good storytelling weather—cool
enough in the evening to enjoy a little fire,

a morning chill
to stir the blood to labor.

Oh, it's not the sun I worship,
but the hour. For now, sit here.

It is a kindness when
old friends can be together, quiet.

This fine October air is ours,
friend, to share. Contemplation

is both our gentlest and
our most awesome power.

At Rexroth's Grave

Off the bluff, white sails wind
among oil rigs pumping the Pacific.

Every grave but Rexroth's
faces toward the sea.

He faces the continent
alone, an old explorer,

hawk-eyed, sharp-tongued,
walking inland with his oar.

Blue Monody

blues for Thomas McGrath

And now the winds return,
blowing in from the sea,
driving summer steadily away,
south toward tall palms
we dreamed of when we were children
shivering in snows
that never ended.

And now these winds return
with frozen hands and laughter,
tormenting mountains,
twisting trees until you think
that like any human heart
they cannot bend farther
and will surely break.

I've kept my heart in my hands
through all these storms and seasons.
I've held it tight.
When the great trees bend
and their groans are almost human,
I've looked up more than once
from the desk where I invent a life,
looked up stunned
when they cried out,
thinking it a friend
arrived for comfort in the cold,
or my own harsh voice
grown suddenly old and fearful,
the fitful cry of a man whose name
was never counted
among the names of the innocent

and now must face the winter.
I've held my heart
in my hands and pushed
my breath across it
to blow the snow away.

Traveling, traveling, I've learned
a few exotic names
and places where great deaths occurred,
where the lonely are buried in their trenches,
in mass graves which couldn't,
under all that earth,
disguise the misery carved
into ordinary faces.

The winds continue to grieve
although the dead ask nothing
from us now. And nothing
is what we gave:
I've held tight
to this heart I could not break
like an egg to eat.

The wounds, the wounds I bore
were not my own,
but this hunger is all mine.

These trees, defeated by the wind,
endure: they cling to the earth
and won't let go
despite sea winds drumming blows.
***

Down in the bay, the old wharf
slowly crumbles,
gray wood bleached almost white,
huge timbers ruptured.

Homer thought a field of lovely asphodels
would mark the homelands of the dead, but we know
differently, having seen
those faces rising from the sea
a thousand times or more,
their own chewed hearts
rotting in their hands, each
inarching slowly inland
with his broken oar.

No matter how far inland we may stray,
we can't escape the sea.
Each heart longs to be
Odysseus, to bear its wounds
forthrightly,

long enough not to survive,
but to embrace,
if only once again,
Penelope.

Here on the gnarled coast, winds
play cruel jokes, twisting trees
into almost human forms
reminding us of nothing
so much as our own brutality.

Cold September winds blow in from the stormy sea.
I've got my heart in my hands again.

If you pass by, do not think that I
am not afraid.
Winds will drive me down beneath the waves,
under ravaged trees I cannot save.

They are neither laurel nor myrtle;
nor am I

a Milton;
nor you
a Lycidas, nor dead.

Here is the wreckage of a heart:
take it from my hands.
No one understands
the winds or the sea. We mourn because
we are alive. I give you this monody.

***

It is true, as the poet sang, Elder Brother:
Every angel terrifies.
I've never seen an angel, but I've beard
those cries of a desperate cat,
bawling with and without her Tom,
the sexual need to scream
the soul's desire, the cries
we all come from…
every angel terrifies. Because
there is also
always a little ugliness inside,
every angel terrifies.

The deep sexual wail of the alley cat
is purest song, uncluttered by metaphor or meaning
it says nothing but what it is—
the single note of desire without cunning,
its only meaning *being*—
We confuse the sound; we have our self-
deceptions to consider, we
who are burdened with enormous
intentions to remember.

Everyone is desperate,
singing solo.

Night comes down hard
and we turn alone in bed
toward bare needs we'd meant
to leave behind.

We listen to the dark
and hear only winds and waves
that never stop. Somewhere
between nightmare and insomnia,
stars conspire to wink and shine.

Old Companero, I tell you,
the thought of singing solo
terrifies:

Bird on the hill,
little cricket
itching in the grass . . .

bitterness like a razor on the tongue . . .
It is hard, brother,
seeing those blank faces
of battered mothers
at the marketplace, hard looking into empty eyes
of children who die
a little every night.

"The soul
to know itself
must look into a soul"
and sing.
There is always
that old eternal
other side of things—
which brings us
to our knees.

A mirror is not a soul. It's not
for daily trivialities,
not even for our own
self-centered lone-
liness that we listen
at the heart of things.

Stoked on drugs
and driving at light speed
down a dead-end street,
there's barely time to think.
What terrifies most deeply
is what we see
inside: every angel
driven out by lies.

Jeezus-gawd-aw-mighty, there were angels
in your eyes!

Imagine Hoover
waking alone in the night,
thinking hard on your fate,
on the fate of your sisters and brothers, Hoover
flat-nosed, square-jawed, no-neck bigot
swirling into vertigo,
nauseous,
choking on his own poison phlegm,
cursing, *"Nigger! Kike!"*
as the faces (black and white)
march past him:
his allies:
the Senator from Wisconsin,
Joe McCarthy, and his cronies,
Bobby Kennedy and Richard Milhous Nixon;

and the House Committee
on Un-
American Activities

—a Commie in every bed,
a socialist in every bath—
and those who made the Blacklist,
not least of all
that proletarian angel, Tom McGrath.

Hoover sweats and clutches his heart
and tries to focus on his night-light.
The angels of dead civil rights
workers march slowly, inevitably, by,
bloody, marching toward breaking daylight in the east.

Confluences, visitations,
demon ghosts of the present arrive here from the past
The Ghost of Christmas Present?

There is no peace.
And every angel terrifies.

***

Is that it?
Carbuncles on the skin of the body
politic?

Ten years ago,
snug in his little house
on this high, wind-blistered bluff,
low fire in the stove despite
it being midsummer
in the Northwest,

Tom McGrath sank deep into his chair
and turned warm eyes
opaquely back on time
to remember thorny years
lost in the depths

of "the hornacle mines,"
winding labyrinths deep beneath
the infected and infesting streets
of the City of Lost Angels
until at last he escaped into
the long bleak night of the frozen north,
leaving Marsh Street and the hornacle mines behind
to entered the thirty-year Christmas
of his wild American dream-dance
imagining a friend.

The Revolution lurched along somewhere
out there among rubbish left behind
by pale men who manned the picket lines.

Times were thin.

He lit a cigarette from a cigarette,
rolled his eyes, and grinned,
"K-e-e-e-rist,
you haven't seen anything
until you've seen the winds sweep Moorhead
after the snow has frozen!
I swear you can *see* the cold!
Gawd, I'd hate to grow old up there."

From hornacle mine to beet-packing plant,
we followed . . .
going down there, over the river,
alone, over the river,
over winter ice.

We were all gloriously lost together,
lost along the way, searching
for a heaven of blue stars, building the Big Kuchina...

And there it is
in the hexagrams
of yesterday's *I Ching*,
there it is,

written in piss in new winter snow beneath a cold blank sky
a thousand miles from nowhere,
a few miles down the road,
over the frozen river,
over winter ice:

To have power over Nature,
to have power over Bird and Forest,
over Sea and Mountain and Wild Beast,
to dream of power,
to cling to the dream of power in the hour
of greatest need—
to have stood silent
is to conspire, is to concede.

And now, a little south of here,
the white train rolls,
the white train regularly rolls.

"To be men, not destroyers,"
that was the task Grampa set,
learning from his own broken heart:
"wrong from the start, that stupid
suburban prejudice."

Stars caught in the bristling bare branches of trees
before the ice storm brought them down,
the earth frozen and black the river
buried in shadow, no longer dreaming
a calm, indifferent sea
a little ice along its banks.
It is time to face front,
get back on the line.

Strands of fog erase this stretch of beach,
swirls of fog erase the sky above the Sound.

To be takers, yes, to be sure;
but to be givers
also; to surrender
The Goods;
to be
searchers for the art
of the sublime—his sermon was the gift
of courage to face front and get back on the line.

Carbuncles on the cold skin
of the Body Politic.
The thin black shadow of a Trident nuclear Sub
slices the vast Pacific.

To be men,
not destroyers,
that's the trick.

***

A gray night, just a few years ago,
we spent hours sipping on a beer,
remembering Michael Harrington,
his body wracked with cancer,
his soft, patient voice over Public Radio
offering every moral answer
to the Reagan/Bush agenda—
marching orders against the Sandinistas—
and we toasted Norman Thomas,
Tom looking me in the eye
and asking how many will die
before the murders end,

and the jukebox of course
played a sad country song,
and he stood unsteadily, leaning on his cane,
and made a bad joke about Pound's posturing—

cane and cape and earring
during his early days in London
("the man wouldn't have been dumber
if he'd posed as Beau Brummel")—
and apologized for the music
"but not for the people—
'drather have a beer in here
than anywhere else in the country."

Dirty floors and haggard faces,
so many dreams pissed away.

Neither disgraced nor enlightened,
these were the men in the trenches,
the women who sent their sons to war,
who worked the factories, who paid taxes.

"Everything's in order," he said, and laughed,
"Some to die, some to be maimed,
everything is ready.
Everything's been done."

We cross the avenue:
"Helluva life when crossing a gutter's
the biggest challenge of the day!"
And he clutched my arm.

[Safe at his desk, door cozily bolted,
stealing a moment, another, higher, poet
peers out his window: two floors below,
the homeless go about their tasks,
and he records his heart to bursting,
he measures out his sympathies
before his lecture on form and epiphany—
probably at the expense of his graduate
seminar on Later Keats.]

The afternoon sun rides high above
the northern Mississippi. A few cars slide by
as we walk slowly
under maple saplings in fluttering leaves
along clipped lawns in an autumn breeze.

Across the street, a man in greasy hand-me-down;
strides by with his sleeping roll.
"That one's been on the road
a while," Tom laughed softly,
"probably tryin' to find a train."

And we are a long way
outside Yellowstone
and a longer way from Port Townsend.
The things we've seen will never come again,
and who'd want to live them over?
And nothing changes. The poor
are the same poor, and the dead and the dying
are the same.

Where is the meaning? "Six million dead"
means nothing to us—we who've only witnessed photos
our abstracted, two-dimensional, superficial
understanding.
And the seven million Russians, Estonians, Latvians
Lithuanians, figures reaching ever-farther beyond
the ability of one mind to grasp?
Don't ask.

"In America," he laughed,
"it is one thing to stand against murder,
and another to do without supper."
We stammer and cuss and blame one another.
The heavens continue to burn.

Somewhere in transit,
somewhere driving toward Pah-Gatzin-Kay or Boston
crossing the Great Mountain, say,

that lies just outside of Moorhead,
the sound of the sea comes back to us
like the voice of long dead sailors,
familiar with its longing,
the hush of Puget Sound
when winds ride bluffs that rise above Fort Worden
and rattle the twisted limbs of brittle old madrona,
white flowers scattering to the winds,
winds,
when they return again each fall,
driving summer steadily away,
when all the winds and rains return with icy fingers…
Homer thought a field of lovely asphodels would mark
the homelands of the dead.

What survives in the heart,
what endures,
lies just beneath what is said
when what is said
is said
just so:
only thus do we know
our own temple, our heaven, home or hell.

Cisco Houston sang,
You don't believe I'm leavin'
You can count the days I'm gone.

***

Yellow alder leaves fall
where madrona blossoms,
small, delicate,
had fallen.

The grass grows tall and brown, and apples
beckon yearling deer

to come down from wooded bluffs
and gorge until they're drunk.
Autumn fog tumbles along the water.
A few boats, a few seagulls—
like an amateur painting.

Sunlight slanting away, turning yellow.
I've been sitting on the deck of the same bar
for hours, ignoring my whiskey,
watching the changing dance of sunlight on the water
as the day or a lifetime passes . . .

And the low whiskey-colored sun,
its clattering light on the water,
my own self-pity
and the cry of the loon and the whine of a gull
and the toot of the out-going ferry.

I hang slack-jawed, empty,
a growing numbness just behind the eyes
although I am stone sober—

. . . sadness, melancholy,
or any of those other insufficient names we give to
grieving,
or any of those other insufficient names we give to living
while the puffins go on diving
and mountains in the distance turn black and then silver
sky growing pale and growing wider.

A shadow grows over me and I shiver.

Poised at the edge of the sea
like a damaged bird, I keep one eye
on each horizon: westward,
the vast implacable ocean
stitched to the wide indifferent sky;

to the east, mountains,
and beyond the mountains,
mountains, and the great rolling plains
where winds of change blow through our lives
like snows across the Dakotas, a cold blank nothing.

From the four corners of exile,
from the cracks and ravines of the ruptured human heart,
from the sea and the shadows of mountains,
a few friendly shadows,
a few friendly faces come back again
to taunt us, to lure us back on the line:

T'ao Ch'ien alone in his cabin
far from the intrigues of the city,
trying to give up the wine,
committed to his garden,
rests only at night to write poems
remembering his home on South Mountain;

sad, wise Tu Fu in exile,
alone at his brushwood gate, waiting to share his wine;
Saigyo gazing alone at the moon,
writing poem after poem;
Basho and Ryokan
alone on Sunset Hill
watching the River of Heaven pour down across Sado,
island of exiles in the Sea of Japan.

And I return to Helen,
exiled in Alexandria
while Troy burned.

Rexroth, exiled in Montecito
after forty years in The City,
wrote his best poems, love songs, elegies and his own epitaph.
What more could you ask?—a lifetime learning to speak simply.

When fame kneeled at the feet
of Georgia O'Keefe, she, saintly, remained silent,
closed her door
and went on painting flower and bone and blank
pale sky, eighty-nine pages on file at the FBI.

Van Gogh, who couldn't peddle a painting,
saw only the same starry sky which demanded
he learn to speak
with his entire body—he too
listening with his eyes.

Down Port Townsend Bay, the paper mill
blows sulfur smoke in columns of soft white cloud
as the evening shift begins.

In town, it grows late.
The bric-a-brac shops and antique dealers,
the Rotary Club and Republican steering committee and
Chamber of Commerce, banks
and city offices close for the night again.
The day's decisions have been made
without the counsel of T'ao Ch'ien.
It's Friday night.
There's a football game.

***

And now the winds return, late,
to torment trees,
blowing autumn in from the sea.
These trees,
defeated by the wind, endure.

Faces rise through the night
as through water,
each with its blessing or its warning
we've heard a thousand times before,

each with its gift of hope and terror
we can't refuse,
each with its questions and its knowledge
while the trees groan or shriek in almost human voices.

Exiled from the Garden,
this is the garden we murder and survive,
listening to days and seasons, to inconstant tides
and our own reflexive lies, refusing
to open our eyes to the enormous tragedy
of waterline and riverbed and darkening sky:

we struggle to re-invent the Garden with insecticides:

Pythagoras thought form reflects
the irrational numerology
of Pure Mind. The Pure Mind of Buddhism
declares this world
illusion.

It is late.
I he world sleeps or rises
or goes about its way. The wind blows.
The sea sighs. Someone once again,
at midnight,
opens the book of the heart.
A tree rattles and groans.

We are not in the dark.
We are not alone.

A Visitation

I wake suddenly, in the middle of the night,
and realize I'm stroking the pillow beside me,
dreaming of my wife who is six months dead.

I rise and brush my teeth and pour a stiff drink
and go out into the garden to sit
on the old iron bench and think.

It's after midnight and the moon is almost full.
And after a long silence, I hear, faintly,
a woman's heels' *chink, chink, chink,*

against the ancient cobblestone
beyond the garden wall
as she makes her way down the street.

Sam Hamill: A Matter of Character

Stephen Kuusisto

When I was a child I spake as a child; then I found poetry. This is the jeu d'esprit of the matter: poetry as innocence, or obversely, if a poet is political, she possesses childish candor. "Mommy, why does the president have yellow teeth?" "Why are those men burning the houses?" By adopting this voice a poet needn't protest her or his innocence. To do so would hint of experience, maturity revealed—proving the poet knows too much. In American poetry it has been best and customary to speak as a child over the past fifty years or so.

We can place Robert Bly's Viet Nam protest poem "The Teeth Mother Naked at Last" in the camp of innocence. Bly famously wrote it was because the aluminum screen door industry was prospering that people were dying in Asia. Even at twenty (when I first encountered these lines) I knew Bly's poem lacked scruple—his emotion was filtered through a childish voice.

With Sam Hamill's passing last spring we lost a mature poet whose voice was never callow. Sam achieved this because of his scholarship—with the exception of Kenneth Rexroth and Gary Snyder I know of no American poet who has read so deeply in Chinese and Japanese poetry and philosophy —not as an avocation but as a critical part of daily practice. In his introduction to The Poetry of Zen he writes:

> *"ZEN IS A MATTER OF CHARACTER, not a matter of intellect,"* as D. T. Suzuki emphasized. And yet there are probably tens of thousands of readers of Zen books for every one who has experienced Zen, which means simply, "meditative absorption." Its practice, its embodiment, is zazen (tso-ch'an in Chinese), "sitting meditation." Without a daily sitting practice, the experience of Zen remains an intellectual exercise. Only through maintaining such a practice may one begin to encounter the true "collectedness of mind and compassionate heart" that leads to self-realization and transcendent wisdom.

It is this "collectedness" I want to talk about—reading, writing, sitting, meditating, these are the collects of poetic and spiritual majority and mastery. From the Japanese poet Basho Hamill learned "each poem is the only poem. Each moment is the only moment in which one can be fully aware."

Consider Hamill's poem "Black Marsh Eclogue":

> Although it is midsummer, the great blue heron
> holds darkest winter in his hunched shoulders,
> those blue-turning-gray clouds
> rising over him like a storm from the Pacific.
>
> He stands in the black marsh
> more monument than bird, a wizened prophet
> returned from a vanished mythology.
> He watches the hearts of things
>
> and does not move or speak. But when
> at last he flies, his great wings
> cover the darkening sky, and slowly,
> as though praying, he lifts, almost motionless,
>
> as he pushes the world away.

The poet watching the hearts of things finds is a shy, unanticipated eschatology. Shy for its unassuming awareness which is both nature itself and whatever we mean by "mind." Shy because the poet eschews spiritual judgment like Walt Whitman's famous animals who do not fret:

> I think I could turn and live with animals,
> they are so placid and self-contain'd,
> I stand and look at them long and long.
>
> They do not sweat and whine about their condition,
> They do not lie awake in the dark and weep for their sins,
> They do not make me sick discussing their duty to God,
> Not one is dissatisfied, not one is demented with the mania of
>   owning things,
> Not one kneels to another, nor to his kind that lived thousands of
>   years ago,
> Not one is respectable or unhappy over the whole earth.

***

Maturity is an unfashionable word. Americans particularly favor modeled childishness. We love our Enfant terribles, our Kerouacs and Ginsburgs. I place Hamill alongside Denise Levertov, Adrienne Rich, Rexroth, and Snyder because they are collectively steeped in the "real work" of overcoming apprehension, disquiet and restlessness. I'm talking here of spiritual shrewdness which, if and when attained, came through considerable pain. Let me close by quoting in full one of Hamill's most remarkable poems:

True Peace

Half broken on that smoky night,
hunched over sake in a serviceman's dive
somewhere in Naha, Okinawa,
nearly fifty years ago,

I read of the Saigon Buddhist monks
who stopped the traffic on a downtown
thoroughfare
so their master, Thich Quang Dúc, could take up
the lotus posture in the middle of the street.
And they baptized him there with gas
and kerosene, and he struck a match
and burst into flame.

That was June, nineteen-sixty-three,
and I was twenty, a U.S. Marine.

The master did not move, did not squirm,
he did not scream
in pain as his body was consumed.

Neither child nor yet a man,
I wondered to my Okinawan friend,
what can it possibly mean
to make such a sacrifice, to give one's life
with such horror, but with dignity and conviction.
How can any man endure such pain
and never cry and never blink.

And my friend said simply, "Thich Quang Dúc
had achieved true peace."

And I knew that night true peace
for me would never come.

Not for me, Nirvana. This suffering world
is mine, mine to suffer in its grief.

Half a century later, I think
of Bô Tát Thich Quang Dúc,
revered as a bodhisattva now—his lifetime
building temples, teaching peace,
and of his death and the statement that it made.

Like Shelley's, his heart refused to burn,
even when they burned his ashes once again
in the crematorium—his generous heart
turned magically to stone.

What is true peace, I cannot know.
A hundred wars have come and gone
as I've grown old. I bear their burdens in my bones.
Mine's the heart that burns
today, mine the thirst, the hunger in the soul.

Old master, old teacher,
what is it that I've learned?

Sam Hamill's Last Poems: A Sampler

After Morning Rain, by Sam Hamill (Tiger Bark Press 2018)

Bob Herz

This is not meant as a critical essay but rather as a sampler of the work in Sam Hamill's posthumous and lovely book about poetry and love and loss and friendship, the issues which drew his attention throughout his career. There are allusions to forebears, to ancient and modern international poets, memories of travel and place, and poems about getting old. The book is sweet and generous, and contains one of my favorite Hamill poems, "Nightingales of Kifissia," previously published here in *Nine Mile Magazine*. It contains none of the great long poems, which made his collected poems, *Habitation Collected Poems* (Lost Horse Press, 2014) so powerful and necessary an addition to anyone's library, but it is an important collection from an important poet.

Sam died on April 14 of this year at age 74 from complications of chronic obstructive pulmonary disease. He lived an extraordinary life. An honorably discharged Marine who became a pacifist, he overcame a heroin habit that began when he was a teenager. He founded Copper Canyon Press in 1972 with three other people, and served as its editor for the three decades, publishing hundreds of books by such poets as Pablo Neruda, Rabindranath Tagore, Octavio Paz, Carolyn Kizer, Ted Kooser, W. S. Merwin, and Marvin Bell. His publication of Kenneth Rexroth's *Collected Poems* rescued that great poet from back-list neglect.

His list of publications as an editor was a product of his belief that the job of the press was not merely to publish books, but to publish great poetry in order to change the world. He sought as an editor and as a poet to publish and write poetry that engaged the world. His Poetry Against The War movement of 2003 was a protest against the military campaign in Iraq that began as a reading at the White House gates. He created a website that attracted more than 20,000 poets, with some of the work eventually collected in *Poets Against the War* (Nation Books, 2003). He left Copper Canyon in 2005 over creative differences, and while the press remains an important publisher of poetry, with his departure it lost that special crusading edge that Hamill brought to it.

His introduction to poetry came from Kenneth Rexroth, a friend who helped him give up drugs and taught him about poetry. "Poetry gave me a reason for being," he once said. "And I'm not exaggerating when I say that. My ethics, my sense of morality, my work ethic, my sense of compassion for suffering humanity, all of that comes directly out of the practice of poetry."

Like Rexroth, he was a celebrated and prolific translator and poet, publishing several books of prose and poetry. *After Morning Rain* is his 18th collection, published posthumously by Tiger Bark Press earlier this year. The book opens with "In The Beginning," a complex aesthetic and linguistic meditation on words and what precedes them, that concludes with the statement that "to evoke is to transform" as an explanation of "the artlessness of art." The heaviness of that description notwithstanding, the poem moves lightly along, a song of itself, a lovely surprise of melody and movement freighted with ideas.

The poems in this book, like "In The Beginning," are all shorter poems, most of them a page or less, only a few more than that. All are strong. I confess to finding that a pleasant surprise. Sam's strengths in prior books have seemed to me to be in his longer poems, where his thought has time to work itself out and his melodies get the space they need to find themselves as his burdens get paid. In this book the action moves quickly even in short pieces:

> When the last spring rain
> strips the rhododendrons
>
> and petals lie scattered at their roots
> bleaching slowly in the sun, turning white,
>
> I sit alone through the long afternoon,
> warm breeze blowing through me,
>
> a whisper of distant bees,
> green world bathed with infinite light.

That is one of six short poems in the first section of the book, all of them about light and transcendence and memory and his garden. Here is another:

> Thirty-one new yellow daffodils
> bloom in the little garden.
>
> Alder seed covers everything
> with little flakes of rust.

A breeze through evergreens.
Distant bird-trills.

When Hui Neng tore up the sutras
his bones were already dust.

The first section of the book opens with a meditation on words and language and what precedes them, and the second section follows in the same mode, opening with a poem called "Theosophy & Geology in the Flesh," which describes a dream and then the end of a dream. It begins with a vision of a bird soaring among the mountains, and continues with an evocation of his dead wife,

And last night, in my sleep,
in my dreams, you rose
like a soft warm star,
your skin barely visible
beneath a gauze chemise,
your brown hair smelling rich
as river valley topsoil.

He speaks of how "old ravens peruse / the transparent pages of heaven" as unseasonable warm weather breaks up the ice in the water and the world waits the fires of spring. There's no shock, no turnabout. This Love, the coming spring, and the dawn, defeat the near-death souls of the nation of the avaricious:

And here, the world ends,
crumbles away in snowy chunks
drifting out across the sea.
And the moribund souls of a nation
of avaricious men grow small,
futilely wan,
in the hard cold light
of tenacious northern dawns.

Section III opens with "Another Year," a poem in which Sam and an imagined Tu Fu drink at midnight with "little to celebrate" as the "capital is overrun and occupied / by human vermin / spreading misery and ecocide." The depressing vision continues with "On the Longest Day of the Year," about a place in which he and his confreres have lived so long in rain that their "totem / is the salmon," and in which "No one here remembers / the ceremonies of the sun." Relief from this gloom comes with the poem "A Friend Speaks of Tibet," which opens by lamenting that

> Tibet is a battered woman,
> a mother under siege,
> struggling to stay alive...

But from this point the poem finds a more salvific voice, ending with the poet feeling the presence of that country's culture and religion, "like finding myself on a journey / I'd forgotten I'd begun." Other beautiful poems follow in this section, remembering Kenneth Rexroth, Gwendolyn Brooks, Takamura Kotaro, and others. In Section IV are several stunning love poems to his dead wife, including one published in *Nine Mile Magazine* which leaves me misty-eyed each time I read it. "Nightingales of Kifissia" seems a good place to end this sampler of Sam's final book:

> An evening in Kifissia, a taverna
> after the botanical garden,
> now more than thirty years ago,
>
> the nightingales, hundreds,
> the sound of nightingales through it all.
> And me feeling terribly alone.
>
> Ten years later, walking with my new wife
> through the teeming streets of Tokyo,
> the convocations of jungle crows,
>
> loud, rude, but sounding
> happy, happy as I was—
> for a little while . . .
>
> Then, ten years ago, my wife
> feeding sparrows at her feet
> in a Buenos Aires plaza, speaking
>
> softly of my life after her death
> by cancer. So much grief in me
> that I found no question

and no answer. She laughed and said,
"You'll have to find yourself
a hottie," and fed

the bird on our table and it hopped
right into her hand. "You see?"
she said. "Love is everywhere."

After years of mourning,
I was awakened one dawn
to the sound of doves

above the empty streets of Paris.
Grown old, infirm, I felt
my heart grow young again,

remembering there is
so much meaning to touching
a hand, a cheek, across a little table,

what it means to speak
intimately of cities and streets,
to tell of how the sparrows eat

in Buenos Aires, and how,
in Kifissia, the nightingales sing
away my grief. While she I barely knew

made coffee, singing softly,
I said nothing
while I thought these things.

Interview With Sam Hamill

Andrea Scarpino

I interviewed Sam Hamill over the course of the 2004 election—the election in which President George W. Bush won his second term in office. Our email exchange began in October and continued through December of that year. I was a graduate student at the time and had spent the summer and fall working to register young women voters in the hopes of keeping Bush from a second term. Volunteers from a national feminist organization were sleeping in my house doing everything they possibly could to move Ohio, one of the famous swing states, away from Bush.

I went to graduate school in poetry in part because I believed so strongly in the power of poetry to change the world—and found myself in a graduate program that valued personal, private poetry over the profound effects that poetry can have on a public's consciousness, on social change. Hamill was a poet I deeply respected and admired for his poetry as well as for his work organizing Poets Against the War, which began as a reaction against First Lady Laura Bush's invitation to attend a White House Symposium called "Poetry and the American Voice" and resulted in a dynamic website of anti-war poems, an anthology, and the resurrection of an anti-war poetic movement. I was ecstatic to have the opportunity to interview Hamill (an opportunity that our own Stephen Kuusisto arranged), but you will undoubtedly notice a clumsiness in my interview questions. This was the first time I had ever done something like interview a famous poet! But I desperately needed to hear Hamill's thoughts on public, political poetry. I desperately needed a famous poet to tell me political poetry was important, was valuable, needed to be written. Especially after Bush was re-elected (or, as I note in my interview, elected for the first time), I was desperate to believe that resistance was possible, and that poetry could have a place in that resistance. Given my graduate program, given the hours I had spent registering voters, seemingly to no effect, given the hours I had spent organizing with other volunteers, I needed to have someone like Sam Hamill remind me that poetry's place in resistance is powerful and important.

As Hamill says at the end of our interview, "What can we poets do? We can turn to our fellow poets, living and dead, for courage, for wisdom. We can reread Howard Zinn and the Federalist Papers and think seriously about what we can do, one human being at a time, to be proud of our country again, to bring this vicious jihad to an end, and to become peacemakers in the world. It all begins at home, one person, one day, one hour at a time." In this equally fraught political landscape some 14 years after our interview, Hamill's words still ring true in my ears, still provide hope and courage and a sense of purpose to my own writing and the need for all our lives to serve the greater goal of peace.

NM: Carolyn Forche writes in the introduction to "Against Forgetting" that the distinction between "personal" and "political" poetry is too limiting; that the categorization of "social" poetry is more appropriate. I'm interested in knowing what you think about these distinctions. Do you conceive of your own work as fitting into any of these categories? Do you see a split between "political" and "personal"?

HAMILL: Well, OF COURSE it's too limiting. The "personal" is very often "political." Plath: "Daddy Daddy, you bastard, I'm through!" Is that not a "feminist" moment of rage? Is it not political/social as well as personal? ALL poetry is social: it's rooted in an oral tradition, so whether one's "audience" is one listener or one million, it doesn't matter that much: poetry is social discourse and all social discourse includes the political, the psychology, the historical, etc, aspects. Whether directly or indirectly, overtly or by inference.

NM: I'm also thinking about the popularity of Poets Against the War. Does this tell us anything about the interests of the reading public? And what does this tell us about certain poets' notions that "political" poetry is sub-standard?

HAMILL: When Mark Strand says (in the New Yorker a year ago, reviewing a big Selected Neruda), "Political poetry has no legs," he's showing his ignorance. Sappho? Political poet. Homer? Political. Catullus? Political. And on and on and on. Neruda's "United Fruit Company" has been translated into nearly 100 languages.

When "The Rule of the Colonels" ended in Greece, they celebrated by having Mikos Theodorakis perform his huge symphonic production of Canto General. In Europe especially, poets often serve in high positions in government.

NM: That's a really great point. Why don't they here?

HAMILL: Teaching is a natural element in the lives of most poets, whether formally at an institution or otherwise. We live is a country that is very often deeply anti-intellectual. Our President brags about not reading. We are a country disengaged from its own history and from the history of the world. How else could the American people have been persuaded on more than 40 occasions since the end of WW II to bomb other countries? Europe has a tradition of a "literate class" that includes writers and philosophers.

NM: I remember clearly a photograph of Robert Frost reading at the inauguration of President Kennedy. I also have very vivid memories of Maya Angelou and Miller Williams reading at President Clinton's inaugurations. These are the only three poets to have read at an American presidential inauguration. Does this tell us anything about poetry's place in the American political world?

HAMILL: The American political environment is, for the most part, corrupt and dishonest and entirely self-serving. The Republocrats are owned and operated by corporations. Mussolini defined the perfection of fascism as the perfect of "the marriage of corporation and state." The Patriot Act is an assault on our Constitution. America went into utter frenzy over a 2-second glimpse of Janet Jackson's nipple while never blinking an eye as we passed 100,000 Iraqi dead in this stupid, destructive war

The role of poets in this culture is to subvert the culture, especially the political culture that finds poets and writers to be so dangerous to the State.

NM: In an interview with Anne-Marie Cusac, you said that poetry is "good at undermining governments and so bad at building them. There's nothing harder to organize than a group of poets." Imagine for a minute a government that IS built by poets, or at least a government interested in our input. What would it look like?

HAMILL: Poets come in almost all stripes, even the occasional fascist, like D'Annunzio or Pound. But most poets are humanists who believe in open minds and the examination of all kinds of ideas. We tend to be very tolerant of minority opinion and suspicious of those who rule. A government influenced by poets would be far, far less war-mongering and far more concentrated on the value of A GOOD LIBERAL EDUCATION in the classical or neo-classical sense. For the moral, mental and emotional health of the nation, as well as for its material prosperity. Tolerance works; diversity works. Education should be thought of as a path to enlightenment, rather than as a path to the goodies.

NM: In the end of your interview, you said, "If you think for one second that Auden believed that poetry makes nothing happen in a real, literal way, then you're a damn fool." Yet in your Open Letter on September 11, 2004, you wrote that "No one, of course, believed for a second that a few thousand American poets could stop this or any other war." So what CAN a few thousand American poets accomplish?

HAMILL: Poetry changes lives one reader at a time, one listener at time. You can't expect large masses of people to suddenly become enlightened overnight. Especially when the messenger is a poet. Poetry is difficult and complex, and that's why its language is so effective.

As social activists, we are among the most articulate and effective of speakers. We contribute to an international dialogue that will, in time, make a difference. It has already made a HUGE difference. Poets around the world have held readings and teach-ins and I have been interviewed by the press in dozens of countries, as have other poets: because we insist upon the urgency and value of poetry AS social engagement. Each poem, each letter, each minute or hour or day spent in the service of poetry and truth and decency is an hour invested in enlightenment, just as sitting zazen is an investment.

NM: In the Nov/Dec (2004) issue of "Poets and Writers," Norman Dubie responds to a question about this being a "golden age for American poetry" by saying, "I think we're the most important nation on the earth right now, because, one: we have thermonuclear weapons, and two: because we have more talented poets than have ever existed on the face of the earth." In an interview with Anne-Maria Cusac, you said, "This is probably the best time for poetry since the T'ang dynasty. All the rest of the world is going to school on American poetry in the Twentieth Century."

And yet, the majority of Americans don't read poetry. How would you respond to Dubie?

HAMILL: If I may substitute "powerful" or "influential" for "important," I think Norman is right. American poetry in the last 100 years has grown as never before. When I was a kid, there were basically no female poets, no black or brown and Asian and Native American poets; there was only the ofay cats in neckties in the academy and a couple of kindly geezers like Sandburg and Frost. Last year there were more than 2000 volumes of poetry published in the USA. All over the world, poets are looking at American poets, just as we American poets have devoured and translated the poetry of the world in the last sixty years.

But for all of our success in the world of poetry, our country remains the biggest threat in the world. Every one of this administration's major actions affects countries everywhere. The arrogance of this government is exceeded only by its ignorance and it is a deliberately calculated ignorance rooted in religious certainty and intolerance every bit as dangerous as Osama Bin Laden's religious certainty.

NM: In an interview with Rebecca Seiferle, you said that poetry "insists upon the long view of things that requires a certain humility before the task at hand." Does this insistence on "the long view of things" as well as on humility contribute to many American's indifference to poetry? We seem to be a nation in love with instant gratification, and humility has never been one of our strong points.

HAMILL: The All-American search for immediate self-gratification could well prove to be our ruin, just as it was the ruin of Rome. Bush is our Caligula. Instead of orgies, he sponsors religious services. The fundamental are the same: a nut-zoid leader with too much power and little common sense and no real humility. His smug countenance is the face of America to the world. How sad. Half this country sees what he is doing and is aghast. Half (the "heartlands") votes on "moral" issues without considering the morality of this war or the essential unfairness of stripping a minority group of people of simple civil rights. Notice how many "blue states" are states with strong international connections . . . states with more immigrants from Europe and Asia.

NM: In "Asphodel, That Greeny Flower," William Carlos Williams writes, "It is difficult/ to get the news from poems/ yet men die miserably every day/ for lack of what is found there." Sometimes we DO get the news from poems—I'm thinking of Wilfred Owen, Forche's El Salvador poems, etc.

Your poem, "Yellow Ribbons, Madness, and Victory" tells us the news, but leaves us with the very haiku-esque lines, "A pale moon at vernal equinox./ Wet snow falls on blossoming daffodils." Why did you end the poem in this way?

HAMILL: A world balanced on the brink of disaster. A cold time for our country. Life is transient and fragile and beautiful nevertheless. Quietness to juxtaposed with the shrill national cry for blood.

NM: You include a poem of your own in the "Poets Against the War" anthology called "Sheepherder Coffee." In that poem, and in much of your work, I'm reminded of Emily Dickinson's advice to "Tell all the Truth but tell it slant--." By leading the reader into "Sheepherder Coffee" with the process of making a cup of coffee, and then circling around to it again in the end, you avoid the criticism often leveled at more overtly "political" poetry that it is too didactic. Have you consciously avoided the didactic by looking at difficult subjects from a slant? Do you think that politically minded poetry leans towards the didactic more often than non-politically minded poetry?

HAMILL: There are ALL KINDS of political poetry. "I think that I shall never see / a thing as lovely as a tree..." Here come the loggers. Here come the "tree-huggers." If I write, "I love you," and "you" happens to be a fellow male, suddenly it's a VERY political love. Tom McGrath used to divide poetry between the "tactical" and the "strategical."

I think all poetry is didactic in one way or another, just as it's nearly impossible to write an "apolitical" poem.

I don't have a conscious strategy when I write a poem. I allow the poem to lead me where it goes.

NM: The election is over, and to my dismay, Bush is again (or for the first time) president. Where do we go from here? What is the next step for poets and activists and activist poets? What is your next step?

HAMILL: The PAW board of directors is expanding and we will be re-organizing for the long haul. We are now well-connected with like-minded poets' organizations around the world, and our job will be to be poets first, that is, to write what is given to us to write; second is our responsibility as poets, as artists whose work is often rooted in daily language, to be truth-tellers, to speak out on behalf of what we care about, whether that be the poetry of social engagement or simply love of the foundations of our country. This administration threatens all of the above and much, much more.

But poetry is a very large house and each of us must be true to our respective Muse. We may stand together against the lies, murders, and profiteering of this administration while still practicing, even enlarging, our diversity.

NM: In your Open Letter published on the Poets Against the War website on September 11th, 2004, you wrote, "If we are to continue past the November election, we must change our name (something like "Poets for Humanity"?) and establish a democratic leadership and enlist new volunteers." Have you thought more about how (and if) to continue Poets Against the War, especially now that Bush will remain in power for four more years? Do you have any plans for another "Poets Against the War" anthology?

HAMILL: Everything is under discussion and much will depend on decisions made over the next couple of months. But Poets Against the War will very likely remain Poets Against the War because that's how we are known around the world and because the "war" in question is not Iraq, it's not even the "war on terrorism," but rather the war on reason and decency and diplomacy authored but this right-wing Christian administration.

NM: I lived and taught in France for a year and a French friend emailed me recently to say that Americans should have a revolution against Bush. Yet Americans seem wary of revolution. What does the rest of the world understand about Bush that Americans don't?

HAMILL: The rest of the world doesn't pee its pants because two guys kiss in public. The rest of the world has neighbors and a sense of history. If we were truly "democratic," Bush would never have gotten to the White House in the first place. Conoco is killing people for oil in Africa, Iceland is being stripped by Alcoa Aluminum, sweat shops are prospering for athletic shoes in south Asia. Horrible governments are kept in power because they serve "American" interests.

What does the world recognize that Americans do not? —That there IS a world and there are consequences for Rule by Business.

NM: My same French friend also wrote me, "There are really two Americas, and unfortunately for the world, the one that is for stupidity over intelligence won." How would you respond to that?

HAMILL: The USA has a two-hundred-year history of votes against its own best interests. We have a long history of racism and homophobia and other forms of social intolerance and a long history of anti-intellectualism. The "moral values" people were more concerned with depriving homosexuals of simple rights of decency than with the slaughter of 100,000 Iraqis and more than 1000 US soldiers and the demolition of a country.

Notice how the "red states" were mostly in this country's interior and south, while the "blue states" are mostly on both coasts and New England. Blue states are more international is perspective and mostly more diverse in population.

We who adamantly oppose this war had NO candidate. We who view the environmental crisis as a major threat to our quality of life and the future of the planet had NO candidate. We who believe in classically "liberal values" had NO candidate. We had no candidate to adequately address the horrors of a Supreme Court dominated by Bush appointees. We had no candidate to stand up and call Bush on his lies; no candidate to respond adequately to the fear-mongering and deliberate deceptions of the Republican propaganda machine. It was really a one-party election in favor of this war and without the courage to adequately address what most threatens our way and quality of life.

Our Constitution is being rewritten. Our election system is controlled by corporations. There are dozens of paid lobbyists in DC for every congressional member and every senator. Our election system for vote-counting is an international embarrassment, a disgrace.

If the USA gives half a damn about the idea of democracy, it had better look long and hard about establishing of a little more of it here.

What can we poets do? We can turn to our fellow poets, living and dead, for courage, for wisdom. We can reread Howard Zinn and the Federalist Papers and think seriously about what we can do, one human being at a time, to be proud of our country again, to bring this vicious jihad to an end, and to become peacemakers in the world. It all begins at home, one person, one day, one hour at a time.

Salaam. Ciao. Pace. Pax. Namaste.

Sam

Philip Memmer

The God of Occupations

It might help if you thought of your task
     the way I think of it,
     poet: you

are a dog, bred for growling
     holy hell
     at anything unusual

in the Kingdom. If you smell something,
     bark and slobber...
     if you hear something,

howl. You're a guard. Why should it matter to you
     if I've left the house?
     And why

should you care, if I put you out
     in the yard? That voice
     could be a robber

or only an angel...
     raise your hackles or wag your tail,
     but do your job.

The God of Balance

It's a fact: I hold your life
    in the palm of my hand.
    Not a metaphor—

my actual palm, your actual life
    and all the others,
    every thing

and room to spare. You can feel it,
    sometimes. You sing of it
    and count yourself

blessed, never once imagining
    the exhaustion
    of a god. I recall

only vaguely the age of rest
    before I forged your world…
    my wrist's long cramp

is older now than light, the strain so great
    I made the angels
    just to hold

my fingers clamped together. One slump
    and a hill collapses…
    one quick twitch

and your oceans spill. Someday—
    it's inevitable—
    I'll let it all go

entirely. Maybe by then
    you'll have ended
    anyway, the small struggles

you work so hard to balance
        long stilled—like a juggler's tools,
        left where they fell…

Or maybe not. Maybe today's the day
        your animals scatter,
        howling,

just before the windows
        start to shake. Waking
        from an unexpected sleep,

I'll wonder why it is my knuckles ache,
        then hear you shatter.
        Forgive me,

but it matters that you know this.
        I'll keep trying. You
        try not to notice.

The God of Erosion

Someday, these red stone hills
        will turn to sand, ferried
        to far distant waters

by that innocuous backyard stream
        you don't know the name of.
        Someone might…

but they'll be gone too, along with
        the red stone houses
        you built on the cliffs,

the gardens and garden paths, the cathedral
        and graveyard and school.
        The stream

will be larger by then…a wide river,
        well known
        to whoever remains…

though who will stay
        once the current has worn away
        both these few stepping stones

and the series of bridges,
        increasingly large,
        your descendants will craft

to replace them? Even now
        you can see the brook
        widening, the near bank

an inch or so closer each year
        to the red stone patio
        you sit at

with a friend and a bottle of wine.
        He's sick, your friend,
        getting thin. You talk

about anything else—sports, your kids,
        or how on the far bank
        some stonework,

long buried, has become exposed.
        The pinnacle
        of some ancient temple,

you decide. *The crowning achievement*
        of a long-dead people,
        he agrees,

vast networks of passages and tombs
        upon which, precariously,
        waits

every single thing you've ever known.
        Too bad, he muses,
        this stream of yours

will wash it away. In the silence that follows
        how loud it is,
        your stream,

even if you don't know its name
        or to where, exactly, it leads.
        Listen:

other gods have suggested
        building boats. The truth is
        by the time your brook

is a threat worth consideration
        you both will be gone.
        But maybe now

you could speak
        of materials and dimensions,
        methods of propulsion,

governance and whiskey storage and pets.
        When your wife
        brings out bread and cheese,

dream up the galley. Just keep him talking.
        Anything
        but destinations,

which you cannot control, and the length
        of the journey,
        which you both can guess.

The God of Driving Alone
in the Middle of the Night

You could be anyone, on your way
          to anywhere…
               doesn't much matter

when you're asleep. And O!
          are you asleep. Despite Coke
          and heavy metal

and the window in January rolled
          half-way down, you
          are out, dreaming

for only-I-know-how-long
          on this dark highway
          so mercifully straight

you might—as a passenger—
          have woken up rested.
          Where are you going?

You're about to remember. But this
          from the start
          was your destination:

this gravel shoulder
          where you're shaking
          and gripping the wheel, praying out loud

to whoever you think might hear.
          Not me, traveler—
          those were my high beams

splitting the road down the middle…
        that was my horn, four screams
        still echoing

with your own. The devil-red glow
        you pant in
        is from my taillights—I'm gone

and I'm not slowing down. Don't follow.
        Someone else
        will have to bless you now.

The God of Wisdom

for Penny Boxall

Seeking me, you begin your climb
   up the mountain:
   at the peak, you believe,

amidst the famous view
   and hard-earned solitude,
   you'll find knowledge. You walk,

and—too soon, you're sure—approach
   what looks like
   the summit: the path leads steeply

straight up into the blue. But
   as you get close, a second pitch
   is revealed,

and beyond that looms a third…though certainly
   that is the summit—
   nothing

beyond that third pitch but the sky.
   Onward, you mutter,
   shouldering your pack…

off you go, into the wind once more.
   How I admire you!
   Up, up you trudge,

though the path turns to ice
   and your bad knees burn…
   you reach that third pitch, and—O!

another crest, obscured behind the last,
    comes into view. You
    climb it, and

another crest, obscured behind the last,
    comes into view. You
    climb it, and

another crest, obscured behind the last,
    comes into view. You
    climb it, and

another crest, obscured behind the last,
    comes into view. You
    climb it, and

another crest, obscured behind the last,
    comes into view. You
    climb it, and

another crest, obscured behind the last,
    comes into view. You
    climb it, and

another crest, obscured behind the last,
    comes into view. You
    climb it, and

another crest, obscured behind the last,
    comes into view. You
    climb it, and

another crest, obscured behind the last,
    comes into view. You
    climb it, and

    *

Fuck this, you spit,
        startling a family of tourists
        eating packed sandwiches

on the latest, fog-shrouded peak.
        And you, too! you hiss,
        flipping off the clouds

and whatever might be behind them.
        You hike back down
        by the shortest route,

and wonder if the pub at the trailhead
        will even serve
        somebody stained

with so much sweat and mud. They will.
        I'm here, where I've always been:
        by myself

in the overstuffed chair by the fire.
        Yes: you stink
        of effort and failure

and faithfulness. Take your boots off
        (if you think you can)
        and buy me a drink.

ABOUT PHILIP MEMMER

Philip Memmer is the author of four books of poems, including *The Storehouses of the Snow* (Lost Horse Press, 2012) and *Lucifer: A Hagiography* (winner of the 2008 Idaho Prize for Poetry, also from Lost Horse Press). The poems included here are from a new book, *Pantheon*, which will be published by Lost Horse Press in early 2019. His work has also appeared in journals such as *Poetry*, *Poetry Northwest*, and *Poetry London*; in the Library of Congress's "Poetry 180" project; and in Ted Kooser's "American Life in Poetry" newspaper column. He serves as executive director of the Arts Branch of the YMCA of Greater Syracuse, where he founded and directs the Downtown Writers Center, and is also associate editor of Tiger Bark Press.

ABOUT THE POEMS

My forthcoming book, *Pantheon*, is a collection of poems in the voices of various imagined gods. I found, after spending most of my third and fourth books talking to or about the gods, that I was interested in letting them finally have their say. I have long considered all of my poems to be persona poems, whether or not they seemed to be in the voice of "Philip Memmer" or a more obviously imagined character... the voice is always a mask, even if it's also undeniable that on some level the voice remains my own. On the other hand, the "you" to whom these various gods speak is, invariably, just me. So there it is: a collection of poems in which (even more than might be typical) the poet talks to himself. I hope, though, that readers will find a place for themselves.

Tom Sheehan

I Who Lost a Brother

I who lost a brother
and nearly lost another
remember the headlines, newsreels,
songs of bond-selling, gas-griping,
and movies too true to hate.

The whole Earth bent inwards,
imploding bombs, bullets, blood,
shrieking some terrible bird cry
in my ears only sleep could lose.

Near sleep I could only remember
the nifty bellbottom blues he wore
in the picture my mother cleaned
and cleaned and cleaned on the altar

of her bureau as if he were the Christ
or the Buddha, but he was out there
in the sun and the sand and the rain
of shells and sounds I came to know

years later moving up from Pusan.
I never really knew about him until
he came home and I saw his sea bag
decorated with his wife's picture,

and a map
and the names
Saipan, Iwo Jima, Kwajalein,
the war.

A Recall for Seamus Heaney

I name myself
walking through the house
before I get there.

On birch floors my shoes
sound dull as wood pulses
an ancient drummer

marked time with.
These dead trees are full
of sassy talk.

A strata of air,
corporeally chilled, moves
a cubit wide in the kitchen,

a polar exercise
taking place.
I have been

other places before,
before I got there:
banging a curragh

against the Atlantic
the long watch
of a day,

wind full of slam
and salt and voice
of the seal;

blackening spuds
in a field fire,
chatting rain alive

on slow coals of sticks
like hiccups, hawthorns
for roofing and stone

markers for walls;
pressed foul as fish
in subterranean passage

with the metallic Atlantic
telling me all its
old stories,

icebergs and whales
and the loan sharks
waiting in the new land;

scavenging a city dump
for furniture, books
and bedding,

waging private wars
against prejudice, hunger,
Roscommon calling me home;

this kitchen, now,
dark-cornered, remote, out
of which I walk toward myself.

Trout Fishing with Rommel's Last-known Foe

The alders went bare above us,
came blue lightning jagged and ragged
        as scars on his arms, the proud chest,
not welts in the beginning but Swastika-
made, bayonet-gathered somewhere
        south of France, high-dry Saharan.

Leaves, forsaken, were false blasts about limbs;
from small explosions came huge expulsions.
        He recalled the remarkable incumbent grace
and energy of grenades, the godness of them, ethereal,
whooshing off to nowhere unless you happened
        to get in their way, conclusively, incisively.

He said, "The taste of shrapnel hangs on like
a pewter key you mouthed as a sassy child,
        a wired can your father drank from which you'd
sneak a few drafts from for yourself in the cellar,
nails you mouth-cached, silvered, lead-painted,
        wetted, iron-on-the-tongue gray-heavy metal

you've only dreamed of since. Yet, where he's come
to since that eventful sand wasn't all he knew.
        On our backs, the bare alder limbs mere
antennae in the late afternoon above us, October's
flies grounded for illustrious moments, the squawk
at our trespass merely a handful of crows

in their magnificent kingdom, he brought home
the last of his brothers, goggle-eyed veteran tankers,
        tinker Tommies under the Union Jack,
raw Senegalese old sentries still worry about,
dry bodies fifty years under mummifying sand,
perhaps put away forever, and then some.

He thinks Egypt has a whole new strain of sleepers
fifty years down the road of their making, the wrap
        of sand as good as Tutankhamen had at hand,
their khaki blouses coming up a detective's work,
a special digger's knowledge, at last citing army,
        corps, division, regiment, battalion, company,

father, brother, son, neighbor, face, eye, lip, hand,
soul, out there on the everlasting shift of sand,
        the stars still falling, angular, apogean, tailing
across somewhere a dark night. Here, our worms, second
place to uniqueness of fashioned flies, keen hackles, are
ready for small orbits, small curves,

huge mouths. And his battles, faded into the high limbs,
a flag run up after all this recapture, say he knows yet
        and ever Egypt's two dark eyes.

Burial for Horsemen

(For my father, blind too early.)

The night we listened to an Oglala life
on records, and shadows remembered
their routes up the railed stairway like
a prairie presence, I stood at your bed

counting the days you had conquered.
The bottlecap moon clattered into your
room in vagrant pieces...jagged blades
needing a strop or wheel for stabbing,

great spearhead chips pale in falling,
necks of smashed jars rasbora bright,
thin flaked edges tossing off the sun.
Under burden of the dread collection,

you sighed and turned in quilted repose
and rolled your hand in mine, searching
for lighting only found in your memory.
In moon's toss I saw the network of your

brain struggling for my face the way you
last saw it, a piece of light falling under
the hooves of a thousand horse ponies,
night campsites riding upward in flames,

the skyline coming legendary.

ABOUT TOM SHEEHAN

Sheehan, Saugus High School 1947; Marianapolis Prep. School 1948; 31st Infantry, Korea 1951-52; Boston College 1952-56. He has published 32 books, has multiple works in *Rosebud, Linnet's Wings, Serving House Journal, Literally Stories, TQR (Total Quality Reading), Copperfield Review, Frontier Tales, East of the Web, Faith-Hope and Fiction, Rope & Wire Magazine, Green Silk Journal,* and many others. He has 33 Pushcart nominations, 5 Best of the Net nominations (one winner). Just

accepted for publication later in the spring is a novel, *The Keating Script.* In production at Pocol Press are these books: *Between Mountain ana River* and *Catch a Wagon to a Star,* both western collections; *Alone, with the Gooa Graces,* a short story collection; and *Jock Poems and Reflection for Propei Bostonians* (prose and poetry of sports in Boston.) *Back Home in Saugus* (a collection) is being considered, as is *Valor's Commission (*a collection of war and post-war tales reflecting the impact of PTSD*).* He was 2016 Writer-in-Residence at *Danse Macabre* in Las Vegas. His latest book, *Beside the Broken Trail,* was released in December 2017 by Pocol Press.

ABOUT THE POEMS

In my 91st year, still somewhat lucky with controllable health conditions, I find my own slogan to always have been, as it is today, "We are born with two things on claim, love and energy, and it is up to us to use them to the utmost, and then some." For me, loss is highly significant, deeply felt, whether it is a son, a parent, a comrade, a once-inspiring teacher, a singular individual worthy of being here longer than he or she has been, or the lilac bush I once man-handled, or a maple tree older than I am which has felt my ax. Even a leaf will turn over.

Ron Riekki

Finding Out Three of Them Lived

dedicated to William Godbey
and to the *Los Angeles Times*

twenty-eight years later

      obsession is a home

         wind

              the ashes from the fire fell horizontal

my wife gets confused—are we speaking about the

      helicopter

      or the

                         plane

ocean

fire

      my PTSD counselor tells me about hers, briefly

      ends with *Let's just say some people should not*

have guns. Her tattoo on her forearm is sick.

I discover a follow-up newspaper article
         archived
                  : three names

                       I feel like I have been vandalized by
                            God with grace
         . . .

Vierge modern

by Edith Södergran (1892-1923)

Jag är ingen kvinna. Jag är ett neutrum.
Jag är ett barn, en page och ett djärvt beslut,
jag är en skrattande strimma av en scharlakanssol...
Jag är ett nät för alla glupska fiskar,
jag är en skål för alla kvinnors ära,
jag är ett steg mot slumpen och fördärvet,
jag är ett språng i friheten och självet...
Jag är blodets viskning i mannens öra,
jag är en själens frossa, köttets längtan och förvägran,
jag är en ingångsskylt till nya paradis.
Jag är en flamma, sökande och käck,
jag är ett vatten, djupt men dristigt upp till knäna,
jag är eld och vatten i ärligt sammanhang på fria villkor...

Modern virgin

I'm not a woman. I'm a neuter, but
I am a child, a page and a bold decision, a bold *beslut*,
I am a laughing glimmer of scarlet sun . . .
I am a net for every greedy fish,
I am a toast to women's honor with
a step towards destruction and chance,
I am a leap into freedom and self and . . .
I'm the whisper of blood in every man's ear,
I am a soul shivering, the flesh, desire and denial,
I'm an entrance sign to the new paradise.
I am a flame, searching, blazing, brazen,
I am water, deep but daring, up to the knees, and
I am free, no terms, no stipulations. I am fire; I am water.

ABOUT RON RIEKKI

Ron Riekki's books include *And Here: 100 Years of Upper Peninsula Writing, 1917-2017, Here: Women Writing on Michigan's Upper Peninsula* (2016 Independent Publisher Book Award Gold Medal Great Lakes Best Regional Fiction and finalist for the Next Generation Indie Book Award), *The Way North: Collected Upper Peninsula New Works* (2014 Michigan Notable Book awarded by the Library of Michigan and finalist for the Eric Hoffer Book Award, Midwest Book Award, Foreword Book of the Year, and Next Generation Indie Book Award), and *U.P.: a novel* (film optioned by Dikenga Films).

ABOUT THE POEMS

I love to do translations. One reason is because they break me out of the ashes of repetition. I like to go to restaurants, ask the waiter or waitress their favorite thing on the menu and then eat that. It makes me try different foods. Translation slows me down to analyze the words of other authors, so I get to be triggered into new ways of thinking. I saw Allen Ginsberg speak in a tent at Naropa and he told the small group of us to "read books backwards." He wanted us to break out of traditional ways of looking at language.

Her poem is stunning. Inspired by her sun, I tried to break out of my standard ways of writing poetry and do something new with my original poem published here.

Joshua Michael Stewart

Jane Kenyon

There's a warm hand on my chest
as I read one of her poems—the one
where she's ten, looking up at clouds,
timothy a halo where she lies. A hand

presses. And everyday birdsongs fly
over her. A life touches life long after
the laws of the physical world play
their role. I read one of her poems

in a clawfoot bathtub in a dark house.
A hand moves up to my head, pushes
it underwater, and when breath

is worth fighting for, but so easy
to let go, the hand raises me
into baptism's iridescent gasp.

Spring Peepers

For George William Myers

So loud, they wake me. My ears clogged
with sleep. Was that a chirp or a squeak?
Is it coming from under the bed?
Did the cat sleek in a bird or mouse?

I nudge the window until it too wakes.
Yesterday it rained, the lawn waterlogged.
And it's from there in that scale model
of the Everglades comes a serenade

not meant for me to transcribe.
These frogs produce a type of antifreeze
within their blood. During winter
they hibernate under logs and loose bark

and become little stones waiting to thaw
back into life to celebrate survival,
to announce it's time to love again, but
before that, there must be some healing.

ABOUT JOSHUA MICHAEL STEWART

Joshua Michael Stewart has had poems published in the *Massachusetts Review, Rattle, The Good Men Project, Atticus Review, Brilliant Corners*, and many others. His first full-length collection of poems, *Break Every String*, was published by Hedgerow Books in 2016. He has worked as a counselor with adults with mental disabilities for close to twenty years. He lives in Ware, Massachusetts. Visit him at www.joshuamichaelstewart.com.

ABOUT THE POEMS

My first book was very autobiographic, a memoir in verse, and though I still write from my personal point of view and experiences, I'm really conscious of the I and am trying to move away from it as much as possible. I've moved away from using metaphor for the same reason, to distance myself further from ego. I've always been focused on the music of the line, but I've been particularly interested in having my lines end in more natural places. I want them to be more wabi-sabi, than Hellenistic, more like trees than Roman pillars. Jane Kenyon, is a very old poem that had an ending that wasn't quite right, and like what often happens a new ending came to me six years later when I was thinking of something else. It is not a surprise that spring peepers made it into one of my poems, but what is new for me is my focus on them rather than them being just background music. Lastly, I like to say things simply as they are experienced and observed. In poetry, as in life, I want to touch and let go.

Howard Faerstein

To The Wary Fox Sparrow
Rustling In The Leaf Litter

I have never given up on you,
Your sporadic visitations.

Live on through the present extinction.
Never abandon me no matter my home.

Visit me in the third month
Of the year of my death.

Visit me again
In the eleventh month.

Always signal the end of winter
As you mark its beginning.

The Wasp and the Unicorn

Wind chimes,
five bells hanging from a rusted unicorn,
house-warming gift from Karen & Ira,
long since divorced,
for Howie & Alice, the same.

It's almost possible to see the fabulous beast
on a summer day when the air is empty
but for light striking the snapdragons,
its goat beard & dollhouse-ladder horn.

Like a hologram
you need to look through it to see it.
Lacking background
there's no foreground.

This morning I watched a wasp
enter the largest bell
and when I stuck a twig behind the clapper
a tiny nest fell out,
a single, circular tier of cells.

Outside the borders of definition
mystery flourishes like lichen,
like blood vessels branching
the rocks & tree trunks.

When the screened porch is open,
say late May: white azalea
already fading, pink one just beginning,
dogwood's green-centered stars
blossoming & the rhododendron peaking,
intoxicating perfume mists the whole house,
the universe as small as my life,
as undiscovered as a unicorn,
the secret of the wasp.

Talking to Myself, I Often Say *We*, as in *We Should Shower Now*

My dead brother sat at the dinner table.

Then we entered the horsetail forest.

Precisely then, honeysuckle became redolent.

My brother spoke of the metronome on our aunt's piano.

The cat spent the night at the foot of the bed.

After the hornet stung my thumb, I heard metronomic buzzing.

I said   *we should wake up now.*

ABOUT HOWARD FAERSTEIN

Howard Faerstein's full-length book of poetry, *Dreaming of the Rain in Brooklyn*, was published in 2013 by Press 53. A second book, *Googootz and Other Poems* is forthcoming from Press 53. His work  can be found in numerous journals including *Great River Review, Nimrod, CutThroat, Off the Coast, Rattle, upstreet, Mudfish* and on-line in *Gris-Gris*, and *Connotation*. He is Associate Poetry Editor of *CutThroat, A Journal of the Arts*, and lives in Florence, Massachusetts.

ABOUT THE POEMS

My poems derive from and are conjured out of my experiences. They are one writer's take on a way of being and surviving as a human being in a beautiful, terrifying and absurd world. These three, all to appear in my new book, *Googootz*, offer a fairly eclectic view of my everyday.

I look at poetry as an assemblage. I'm doing carpentry, taking separate pieces and building something whole. One of my favorite writers, Gabriel García Márquez, said, 'All literature is carpentry,' and I think that's right.

Norma Jenckes

Ghazal Tell Their Last Story

Ibn Khaldun laments the death of his mother and father
in the Black Death of Tunis 1348

The voices of existence in the land tell their last story
The cry of lives faced with oblivion yell their last story.

Stop us, end me, finish it, the dying scream in agony;
plague answers: I hear. I come, I quell their last story.

I bring these fleas, these rats, crowns will roll and glitter
in the gutter. Me you cannot repel—their last story.

Veils torn brutally from the faces of good women (my mother,
O my sister) expose the buboes they spell their last story.

The bubo behind the ear, in the armpit, the groin
Where they hide those dark blotches, that smell—their last story.

You cannot stop yourself? A flea will halt you.
Hide in the miasma of your sighs to knell their last story.

What of Mecca and the Prophet's promise: no disease
would enter there. But Pilgrims fell, their last story.

 Perhaps it's enough that Medina was untouched
God's will: my teachers, my holy parents; I re-tell their last story.

Write it down, Norma, the end of all things human is tears.
God spares no one; He is the only Victor to excel their last story.

Ghazal The Funhouse Mirror of Time

Like a fish on a line I wriggle when I look in the mirror;
caught me up short, but there is no hook in the mirror.

My saints, my guardian angel, my confessor,
his counsel – what else did I overlook in the mirror?

Where to find all those friends and lovers who stare
back at you; those you forsook, in the mirror.

You sought safety, shelter, your comfort zone;
but there is no private nook in the mirror.

The book, the calls home, the hospice visits; recount
all those broken vows that you undertook in the mirror.

He finished off the vodka, the beers were long gone
when he noticed how his hand shook in the mirror.

Lord Jim, Anna Karenina, Othello, those never
fail to move you – to them I raise my book in the mirror.

Then there's the day that you grasp the fact
that even you hate how you look in the mirror.

We argue, kiss and argue again the same battles
like caged birds who peck at the rook in the mirror.

Sans teeth, sans mind, sans hair, sans everything--
that glass shows us what time took in the mirror .

I'm not sure who's to blame for my losses,
but I seem to spy a crook in the mirror.

"by brooks too broad for leaping" you'll never guess
not leaping lads, but I found that brook in the mirror.

"Oh, Norma, whatever you do, stay in school!"
My mother yelled when I looked in the mirror.

I glimpse a bent form in a store window passing;
I shudder, turn away. Don't make me look in a mirror.

Ghazal In The Sun

Blue pool water refracts light in my window pane in the sun;
as heliotrope, phlox, day lilies wax and wane in the sun.

When the soil pours down our throats, who will count
how many hours or days any of us have lain in the sun?

Brand new dark blue Volvo sits in my driveway
that pitch pines and swooping gulls stain in the sun.

She travels to Palm Beach tomorrow to throw, give
or take away all that Natasha's beauty had slain in the sun.

My three apple trees have round green orbs; I will be gone
when deer come in snow to feast: my loss, their gain in the sun.

It may be true as Shaw says "Money must be made in the dark"
but once he shines the light of his wit, all must explain in the sun.

From the tree over the garage roof and along the deck railing,
a squirrel stops to chatter and flash its russet mane in the sun.

Do I have time to soak seeds, nick their hard shells, set twine ladders,
raise up moon flowers, morning glories to reign in the sun?

Last night in a dream I met the goddess Athena, she shouted,
"You fool, Norma" I left Aphrodite with disdain in the sun.

When I pluck the fragrant lily Star Gazer, I want to place
it on your grave. Would its musk seem profane in the sun?

The Caravan Moves On Ghazal

and let us run with patience the race that is set before us. -Hebrews 12:1

When I told you about an office gossip remark: the caravan moves on.
What do you mean? You expanded— Dogs bark, the caravan moves on.

Some of your pithy proverbs —folk wisdom in Punjabi or Urdu—
once I considered them I saw they hit the mark: the caravan moves on.

If gold rusts, you asked, what will silver do? If the best decays?
If Trump betrays? That ending is stark—the caravan moves on.

Every rope is a snake in the dark, you told me
when I feared our "friend" was a narc- the caravan moves on.

You ran the table, Norma, now finish the race, you forgot the cloud
of witness. I get it now —what a lark—the caravan moves on.

ABOUT NORMA COLEMAN JENCKES

Norma Coleman Jenckes, born and raised in Pawtucket, RI, earned her PhD, (Illinois 1974) in Dramatic Literature and taught at Bryant University, University of Cincinnati, and Union Institute and University. She founded and edited for 19 years the journal *American Drama* and published extensively on Bernard Shaw, Edward Albee, and Canadian theatre.. A poet and playwright, Jenckes has several produced plays and published her poems in such journals as *Ambit, The Paris Review , Antigonish Review, Appalachian Heritage, Origami Project, Eastern Structures* and  others. She has published a volume of poetry *Dementia: That Undiscovered Country.* A Yaddo Fellow and a Fulbright Senior Scholar, she has taught and lived in Ireland, India and Romania.

ABOUT THE POEMS

My interest in the ghazal originated in 1975-76, the year that I spent in Amritsar in India. My husband who is a Punjabi, had accepted an invitation to chair the Department of English in the new Guru Nanak Dev University. There in faculty and student get-togethers I saw that poetry was recited from memory and that people had many couplets stored in their memories for these social occasions. In a funny way it reminded me of times when my mother and I found our relatives in County Tyrone and we were part of many social evenings in various cottages on the Banks of Lough Neagh. There people were called on to sing or recite some famous speech or poem -- their party piece. I recited what I could recall of poems by the favorites of childhood like Yeats, Noyes, Houseman and Byron. The poems that I heard in India were different—they were not in English. They were in Urdu, a language that was displaced in India by Hindi after Partition. I was in the city of Amritsar in Punjab where the community memory of poetry was in Urdu and written by Muslim poets in a form that came from ancient Persia.

I was in my early 30s then and wrote in the modernist style of poetry in free verse. People spoke with great affection of one poet who had lived and taught college in Amritsar, his name Faiz Ahmed Faiz I wrote poems about my year long experience of India and when I returned to the US I published a few of them. But no ghazals.

However, I did begin reading ghazals and especially the work of Ghalib, Rumi and Faiz. Because he was a 20ᵗʰ century poet Faiz particularly interested me. I did not try to write in the form—I was not a formal poet. My husband Yashdip introduced me to the work of Ghalib, his favorite. He would recite couplets in Urdu and laugh to himself. I tried to get him to tell me what was funny. He would translate word for word, but I did not get the joke.

Two books that were published helped me to understand the wit and irony of the ghazals of Ghalib. *Ghazals of Ghalib* edited by Aijaz Ahmad (1971) and the *Oxford India Edition Of Ghalib Life, Letters and Journals* edited by Ralph Russell (2003). Ahmad's book is a collection of versions of Ghalib's work by several contemporary poets in English. He includes the poem in its original Urdu and adds a verse by verse explanation of each couplet. That combination enabled me to listen as my husband translated from the Urdu each couplet. I could then notice where he laughed and then read their renditions of that same couplet by poets and the explanation by Ahmad. Then I could experience a little of what was lost in translation. Mostly it was a matter of humor and tone. And that is a lot to lose.

Then luckily the poet Agha Shaheed Ali was invited to read at the University of Cincinnati. After he was solemnly introduced, he responded with a joke—something like – "Oh here I am in Cincinnati—the city of two sins – how I would like to give you one more tonight." Then is his reading he created a larger sense of what is possible in the range of poetic subject and in the use of the refrain at the end of each couplet and the internal rhyme in each.

Inspired and excited by his example, I began trying to write ghazals. I was immediately surprised by what I came up with. It is as if the refrain is a kind of railroad station that I must pull into at the end of each couplet, and the rhyme word is the portal that allows entry . So creatively I have a map with the start and the destination clear and definite, my unconscious mind devises the twists and turns and revelations to get us there.

Sometimes I laugh when I see where we traveled to get where we needed to go.

Gloria Heffernan

Adirondack Morning Meditation

Eight women tread a late summer trail.
Pine needles and moss muffle our steps.

We have made a pact.
No talking for this one sacred hour.

In the distance the burble of a stream
penetrates the thick-barked bank of trees.

A woodpecker taps out his own Morse Code
while a red squirrel translates from a birch branch.

We tap each other's shoulders pointing mutely at
a bouquet of red-tinged mushrooms blooming

in a twist of pine roots like a fist full of peonies,
poisonous probably, but lovely in the morning light.

At a bend in the trail, we linger on a footbridge
listening to dragonflies darting past our ears.

How hard it is to swallow the sound of awe
as it rises in our throats.

ABOUT GLORIA HEFFERNAN

Gloria Heffernan's upcoming poetry collection, *What the Gratitude List Said to the Bucket List* will be published by New York Quarterly Books in 2019. Her chapbook, *Some of Our Parts*, was published by Finishing Line Press. In addition, her work has appeared in over fifty journals including *Chautauqua Literary Journal, Stone Canoe, Main Street Rag, Columbia Review, Louisville Review*, and *The Healing Muse*. Gloria is an adjunct instructor at Le Moyne College in Syracuse, New York, and holds a Master's Degree from New York University.

ABOUT THE POEM

This poem grew out of a retreat that I facilitated with my Poetry as a Spiritual Practice workshop. The theme of the workshop is defying gravity. We write and read poetry that lifts us up in the midst of the chaos and turmoil in the world that works so hard to push us down. We don't ignore the troubles of the world, but we seek balance as we also appreciate the blessings that abound. The workshop has been running for two years and we are grateful for the opportunity to continue defying gravity together.

Jennifer Whalen

The World Will Not Meet You Here

The world will not meet you here
where weeds bend from walkways
& wind teases to flutter fabric away,
but you can always turn to the world.
Waiting for the sun to lower or a feeling
to hold, you perfected patience
to stillness—was this not what you wanted?
Huddled in an overcoat, whiffs still wander
through walls where you are;
there is no covering grand enough.
Some nights feel as worlds
without effort: they arrive as if rewards
for clinging so diligently to your memory.
Words were rung out on you
but never in sounds stern enough,
so they pierced your guilt but never your reason.
You cannot think a route back to devotion.
Here, somewhere, dried rose petals
scattered to remind that crisping a surface
reveals so little of within. The world
will not meet you here where the music chooses
itself & there is always some silver new
& shiny to tarnish. You were right to be weary
of loving so rickety & without outcome
that the self drains thin—but dearling,
shouldn't the world just once
fill you with fever enough
to fire? Wisdom will not greet you here
where the stairs have railings
& the rooms no balconies to fall.
Caution will take you somewhere safe
& in that bathhouse of vigilance, this streetcar

of exceptional direction, time is too wide
to marvel; the days, too long to stay.

To Better Describe It

The night—shameless thing brightened
by breaking plates & dying
candles—came less like a thief
& more like a grief counselor
on a TV set where an actress recently passed.
Not that it was a particularly somber evening
or callous morning. Not that it wished
to be reversed, but longed
to be remembered at its most endearing.

A clank of a glass scurried all useless noises away.
I forgot the sound of running water,
pages turning, creasing
into companions. The smell of it
was the crisp of after-rain,
but it hadn't rained in weeks.
Not that I was crazy,
but the night had smoothed itself
in such a way the impossible was possible again.

When I realized the lack of effort
it could take to sustain such a feeling,
I started touching: first, the bar top, sticky,
then smooth. Next, curtains laced
inside windows. Then I moved to crowd-people,
twirling inwards, then out. My limbs turned airy
to compact into so many memories;
I still search for words to better describe it.

When asked, I invented professions,
becoming a person
who tests hard, gelatin candies, sucking
until my lips are cherry red,
then berry blue. The night's refrain
now a nascence of proof: a spun-out dance

where it is easy to lie when surely
there was a time I could have been anything,
but I ended up as this.

It's Nine

I am always elsewhere even
when here. Like the procession of a band
of drummers, sticks rapping snares,

we run roads to our rightful
setting. Not that where we happened
before wasn't formal or true,

but how tempting to think
our new aim is the proper place to be.
Is it unfair to take shape?

if half the size, think how many
could swarm this room, breathe this perfume.
Bodies enchant other bodies;

so little to lament
without: no tardiness, no gluttony—
will the clock ever chime nine

& I sink darkly into
& not through? Someone's groping the ground
for car keys; someone's fallen

rich & full in love
with a piano's frequencies.
Their spectacle, a gift

we, the stationary, get to see.
I want to admire this anatomy
for its feeling, not its reason—

these arms, our legs' memory
of billows to carry beat. Most beings
don't need records of evening

to keep on being: trees
tussling their leaves, nuzzling high atop
the heat, their bodies rocking

their heads; I can listen.

It's Twelve

Sleep is too dense, like losing
oneself in suburban sprawl. Falling
into it is like waiting for day

to find purpose. The city
reminds with too little being. It holds
no weight; the noises

it makes compare to other
noises. If we keep moving here
to there with so little

settling, few things will cling.
Tetherless is both frightening
& freeing; solid & liquid

weigh just the same.
Cars find speed outside the window.
If probability holds,

I've met hundreds
of believers, at least one is believing
me. Simplicity can't be

a thwart to invention.
Something must enhance from plain
devotion: the day

to a teacup, night to the saucer
sustaining it—staring still
without turning it underneath

or testing its volume.
The ceiling is shallow; it confines
a whole litany

of memory—how we keep loving
with such balance: just enough weight
for impression, just enough

room to flee. A single down feather
finds its flutter, & it's still
too early for sleep.

ABOUT JENNIFER WHALEN

Jennifer Whalen's poems can be found or are forthcoming in *Gulf Coast, Southern Indiana Review, New South, Cimarron Review, Grist,* & elsewhere. She was the 2015-2016 L.D. & LaVerne Harrell Clark House writer-in-residence at Texas State University. She currently teaches English at the University of Illinois Springfield.

ABOUT THE POEMS

Beginning in 2013, many of my poems began exploring nighttime as a fertile place to explore how the self interacts with others and the exterior world in pursuit of meaningful connection. As with many of the poems included here in *Nine Mile*, my speaker often finds herself in a nighttime social gathering of some kind and attempts to be both attentive to her own thoughts and reactions, as well as to the world around her. I'm also interested in the exterior world's impact on the self's interior (as opposed to the self solely musing on the world), which can be seen most directly in "It's Nine" & "It's Twelve," where the speaker contemplates how different times of night are associated with different activities and actions, and in turn inspire different emotional reactions from her.

While these four poems utilize different line and stanza lengths, each poem uses similar syntax and musicality to help depict a fluid stream of thought and to draw connections between ideas and images. Each of these poems is also grounded in the mental (and emotional) processes of contemplation and depiction, exploring what can be gained from examining one's own thoughts as well as what can be gained from taking the time to attempt to describe or depict the mind's movements to another. As "To Better Describe It" attempts to describe the night by placing it on a spectrum of what it is not like and what it is like, these poems often depict description as an act of expansion, inviting more comparisons and angles into the poem in hopes of a more precise depiction of idea or emotion.

Bill Schulz

Fountains and Shadows

You seek comfort, I know, but
your mother's gone

and her house, a tiny widow's
cottage, hides in a bed

of bittersweet, rosemary,
and the slight shadow

of a passing crow.

Oh, how this house
would glow every morning.

When you say good bye
the sun is up and flocks

of quiet birds cloud the sky.

And this is where our road turns,
by the lake like a mirage

under an autumn sky,
fish so hungry they're

frenzied following a spray
of mayflies, where once you said

Poppy, Poppy look!
It's a fountain of a day.

On the Feast of St. James the Greater
(for Joe C.)

This is where
he would have fished

imagine
him in the dark

gathering gear
stripers transfiguring

the moon's
light he loses

all balance and
bearings thunder

muffling the dry
night sky

what we heard
is in the mist

blowing over
Ram Island

disappearing
like walks

we'll never take

A Consistent Response to The Impossible
(Maranacook Lake, May 2018)

      you will recall
a lake   glass still
and   sunrise

  loons glide
   slight waves
of   cloud bloom

on the shore
  a slight man
   whispers   this

  not   this

  dividing
      the air
with his hand

      and
      the long clouds
      flip

and
  pine boughs
dance

  and you will
believe
you will

Shaker Village, April 2018

(For A.C)

clouds lift
and settle

mist painting
orchards

and sheep warm
under barely

green
apple trees

hungry
when you kneel

drawn to
the grace

in your
open hands

ABOUT BILL SCHULZ

I hold Master's Degrees in English from the poetry workshop at the University of New Hampshire and in Theology from the Franciscan School of Theology. My poems have been published by *The Seneca Review*, *The Kansas Quarterly*, *Nine Mile*, and other publications. Not that long ago I moved like a fugitive on buses and BART trains in the Bay Area. I was hoping to shake off some fears and delusions and maybe learn to surf or play guitar. I studied theology, for God's sake. I lived in Yehudi Menuhin's childhood home in San Francisco, just down the hill from Alamo Square towards the Fillmore. I moved across the bay to Berkeley, close to the Oakland line. I eventually moved back to Portland, Maine, my birthplace on the edge of the Atlantic where I endure the winters and fret about the short summers enough not to enjoy them. I'll always be homesick for California and the Oakland/Berkeley line.

ABOUT THE POEMS

I do a lot of drawing when I am not writing. This past winter I set myself the task of drawing tiny landscapes and seascapes – sprawling vistas shrunk to miniature, pine trees the size of commas. The madness of winter nights? Sure. And this madness spilled into these poems.

My writing has never approached epic expanses. Even so, lately I find myself parsing words like each one comes with a Lamborghini price tag. In these four poems, you'll read many one and two word lines. The longest line is seven words long.

I ask a lot of each word.

These poems are studies of loss, regret, recovery, and grace.

Pesach Rotem

Ripple

With thanks to the Israel Nature and Parks Authority, the Grateful Dead, and Haim Watzman

"And the spirit of God moved upon the face of the waters." —*Genesis 1:2*

I was walking
On the wooden footbridge
Over the marshes
In the Hula Nature Reserve
One late-summer Friday morning
When I looked down and saw a
Ripple in still water.

I was astonished.

What, I wondered, could it be?
What could produce a
Ripple in still water
When there is no pebble tossed
Nor wind to blow?

I pondered the question.

It must, I reckoned, be
The spirit of God
Moving upon the face of the water.

What else could it be,

Here,
In the African-Syrian Rift,
The crack in the Earth

Into which the Heavens
Pour their secrets,

And now,
In the month of Elul,
When the King is in the field
And the Divine Presence is accessible
To all who yearn to be touched by It?

I trembled in awe.

And a turtle poked his head up
From under the water
And grinned.

ABOUT PESACH ROTEM

Pesach Rotem was born and raised in New York and now lives in the village of Yodfat in northern Israel. He received his B.A. from Princeton University and his J.D. from St. John's University.  His poems have been published in more than a dozen literary journals including *Chiron Review, Natural Bridge, Voices Israel,* and *Poets Reading the News.*

ABOUT THE POEMS

The esteemed ursine philosopher Winnie the Pooh said "Poetry and Hums aren't things which you get, they're things which get *you*. All you can do is to go where they can find you." My poetry comes to get me from many different places: snatches of overheard conversation; long-suppressed memories that bubble suddenly to the surface; books and newspaper articles; the rock I stubbed my toe on; the cute waitress at the donut shop. The poetry comes to get me at unpredictable intervals, so I try to be always accessible with a ballpoint pen, a spiral notebook, and an open mind. And when a poem does succeed to find me, it feels like a miracle. Every time.

Some Translations

Bob Herz

My effort is to give a sense of the spirit of the poems, to show why I find them so interesting, hoping that the reader finds enough to like in these versions to then seek the originals.

Ezra Pound had a theory of translation similar to this. A summary of his approach is from Dr. Philip Irving Mitchell (https://www3.dbu.edu/mitchell/poundtra.htm):

1. A true translation must reject "Wardour-Street English," the pseudo-archaic language of Victorian translators. Pound experimented with a variety of poetic style and diction, making free-verse translations of classical works acceptable.

2. Each translation is a kind of criticism of the original. It stresses the strengths of the original, but it also shows what its limits may have been.

3. No translation has to reproduce all aspects of the original. It can choose to concentrate on only some aspects. It can leave part of the original out. It may even add to it or rearrange it in order to accomplish the translator's purpose.

4. Modern topical allusions may be used to bring across the emotions associated with the original's allusions.

5. Translations should be new poems in their own right. They should be artistically well-done.

6. History is a product of the present. All knowledge of the past is experienced in our current reception and reading of it. In this sense, all translation is both a continuity and a re-reading of past texts and authors.

I like this approach, and believe it is better for the translator, and as well for the reader, than metaphrase or paraphrase, which so often result in dead language that does little to illumine the joys and virtues of the original.

1. Anonymous, "Pervigilium Veneris"

Two lines in this 93-line odd poem of unknown authorship written sometime between the 1st and 4th centuries have drawn translators great and bad—from Thomas Parnell, Ezra Pound, Allen Tate, to academic professors, and many others. The lines are: *Cras amet qui nunquam amati / Quique amavit tras ame,* which I translate as "Let whoever has not loved, love tomorrow / Whoever has loved, love tomorrow," but which others treat differently. Allen Tate, a good poet, produced the nearly incomprehensible *Tomorrow may loveless, may lover tomorrow make love*, while Arthur Quiller-Couch's *Now learn ye to love who loved never— now ye who have loved, love anew!* and *Let the loveless love tomorrow, let the lover love again*, by J. F. Pobson, M.A., a professor of Greek, seem to me to show much of the translator's burden but little of love. Walter Pater produced many syrupy pages in his *Marius the Epicurean*, speculating on origin and context. My full version is different from all of these, and takes liberties with the poem's arrangement, shortening stanzas, dropping some of the structure. Such rough handling aside, it is a wonderful poem, and even if you're satisfied with the version here, I urge you to go back to the marvelous original.

Some background on the poem: It survives in two manuscripts, both unfortunately corrupt, each different in the ordering of the work. The time of the poem is early spring, the eve of the three-night festival of Venus (April 1–3). It describes the annual awakening of the vegetable and animal world through the intercession of Venus, an awakening that contrasts with the speaker's isolation and loneliness. Some critics believe the poem was written in the reign of Hadrian (A.D. 117–138) by Publius Annius Florus, historian, rhetorician, and poet, though their dating may rely more on wishful thinking than evidentiary proof, prompted by when it seems the poem *should* have been written, because Hadrian designated as an official state religion the spring ritual of the Greek cult of Venus Genetrix, whom the poem celebrates as the principle of sexual reproduction in nature. Others claim stylistic evidence for later dating in the poem's similarity to such later poems as the *Eclogues* of Nemesianus of Carthage (*circa* A.D. 285), or fragments of Tiberianus, particularly "Amnis Ibat" (around A.D. 350), whose scansion is trochaic tetrameter, not the quantitative syllablics of most Latin poetry at that time. Such dating has led to claims that the poem shows evidence of an historic change in sensibility, the pivot point when Latin poetry began its change to medieval. The focus on the natural world in opposition to the corrupt metropolitan world is also said to be new in Roman poetry, and is seen as further evidence of the the transition to medieval poetry.

2. André Breton, "L'Union libre" ("Free Union")

Andre Breton (1896-1966), writer, poet, anti-fascist, influenced many other French poets, including Yves Bonnefoy and Louis Aragon, whose work is included in this issue of the magazine. Breton is a founder of surrealism, which he defined in his 1924 *Surrealist Manifesto* as "Psychic automatism in its pure state, by which one proposes to express—verbally, by means of the written word, or in any other manner—the actual functioning of thought. Dictated by thought, in the absence of any control exercised by reason, exempt from any aesthetic or moral concern." (There is more to this story of the definition of surrealism, and it is fierce: Breton and his group fought for the rights to the term surrealism with another group led by Yvan Goll, so passionately that at one point the two groups fought publicly. The quarrel ended with Breton's victory, but from its birth surrealism was marked by similar fractures and resignations.)

"L'Union libre" was written in the early 1920's as Breton was developing his versions of automatic writing and "surrealist automatism" techniques as a way to give the subconscious self a kind of moral dominance in a world that seemed shattered by the violence and senseless losses of World War I. Dada-ism, which he and others first embraced, had proved finally nihilistic and unrewarding. The "Free Union" of the poem's title is intended to apply not only to freedom to love without restraint but also the freedom to associate words and images, as Breton celebrates his wife's body in an audacious assortment of images, from wood burning fires and lightning to greenhouses, otters, sandstone, asbestos, broken glass, and more. The method deconstructs her body, making it part of everything, and everything a part of her body, and in the process makes the woman and the poem somehow impersonal—for at the poem's end we know nothing about the woman, not even her name, or what she looks like, thinks, or wants. We feel her only as a force, feel her impact on the poet. Think for example of the images in the first two lines, her "wood-burning hair" and her thoughts that are "summer lightning," and how odd it is that these powerful, active images are what first comes to the poet's pen as descriptions of her rather than, say, her voice or her tenderness, or her face.

Translating this I found myself wondering if this is a love poem, or if it could be considered as one, and if so, how. Does the poet love her? It's hard to tell from what we see here, for the poem seems to be less about love or marriage to a particular person (outside the repeated use of the possessive "my" with "wife," which is an assertion of ownership and not of affection) than a demonstration of the uses of language to describe the other, this unnamed nominal person who is the subject of the poem. If it is not a love-poem in any usual sense, it is certainly a poem in which great energy expended in this effort, a sort of verbal mating dance without end, a psalm of frenetic admiration and regard, in which the language abilities and energies of the poet are on full display in a kind of other-directed showing off; but whatever this is, I don't feel it as love of the other. I'm fascinated by the poem in a kind of push-pull way that leaves me attracted and repulsed. And I think that Allen Ginsberg got it right in his description of the poem:

His list is about his wife, which should be a serious subject and should, presumably, evoke all sorts of nostalgic and sentimental, or romantic, faithful, or sincere improvisations, but what you get is a real twentieth-century dissonance and absolute reliance on the unconscious. And so it's a portrait of his wife, sort of Cubist (in the sense of, from a lot of different angles) but, at the same time, absolutely ridiculous, and even ugly at times, and then, at other times, very romantic and exquisite.

3. Louis Aragon, "Elsa at the Mirror"

Louis Aragon (1897–1982) was one of the leading voices of the surrealist movement in France, co-founding with Andre Breton and Philippe Soupault the surrealist review *Literature*. He was also a novelist and editor, a long-time member of the Communist Party, and a member of the Academie Goncourt. A hero of the World War II resistance in France, he was awarded the Croix de guerre and the military medal for bravery. Following the war he became a leading communist intellectual, winning the Lenin Peace Prize in 1956. He was nominated for a Nobel Prize in Literature four times between 1959 and 1965.

Aragon was basically a moralist whose early infatuation with Dadaism was aimed at exposing what he regarded as the corruption and moral bankruptcy of a world that had engaged in the terror of World War I. Finding Dadaism sterile—being against things does not make you for anything, or give anything to build a life upon—Aragon pursued an interest in the subconscious as a way of suppressing the mental censors that he believed work against free expression, and thus came eventually to Surrealism as a moral and aesthetic position. As he developed, he saw that immense social changes would be necessary to free the imagination of society, a position that led many poets and writers at the time to the French Communist Party, which promised such a world-changing revolution. He did not remain a surrealist, but he kept much of the freedom he discovered in his practice of it for his later poetic development.

"Elsa at the Mirror" is part of a passionate cycle of poems from the *Eyes of Elsa* (1942), named for his wife, Elsa Triolet, who was the sister-in-law of the Russian poet Vladimir Mayakovsky. He saw her as a "woman of the future," an intellectual and social equal, and something more, an inspiration. In these poems Aragon, an atheist, associates Elsa with a form of transcendence, not as a religious awakening, but as a human and aesthetic bridge to the other world. He said that his aim was not deification of Elsa, but the replacement of the transcendent God of traditional religions with a "real" object, a woman of flesh and blood who could serve as his partner in building the future. Aragon celebrated this love in countless poems over forty years of writings. His intensity and ardor never let up; some of the most ecstatic of his love poems were written when the two were in their sixties.

4. Yves Bonnefoy, "Theater"

Yves Bonnefoy (1923-2016) is, says the *Encyclopedia Britannica*, "perhaps the most important French poet of the latter half of the 20th century." The *Britannica* is hardly alone in such praise, as many other journals and critics said the same. To Bonnefoy's credit, he was healthily dubious about such titles and ranking, telling *The Paris Review* in 1994 (The Art of Poetry No. 69) that "One should not call oneself a poet. It would be pretentious. It would mean that one has resolved the problems poetry presents. Poet is a word one can use when speaking of others, if one admires them sufficiently. If someone asks me what I do, I say I'm a critic, or a historian."

Bonnefoy's 1953 book *On the Motion and Immobility of Douve* won him immediate recognition as a major poetic voice. His other books appeared irregularly, interspersed with critical works, and translations of Shakespeare's major plays and of the poems of John Donne and W. B. Yeats. He was impressed by the work of Andre Breton. Like Breton, he believed that dreaming plays a vital role in the creative process, since "writing, and even speaking, in the most ordinary sense of the word, means dreaming..." His 2011 award from the Griffin Trust for Excellence in Poetry's Lifetime Recognition Award says,

> *With his extraordinary book,* Du movement et de l'immobilité de Douve, *published in 1953, he embarked upon an original and luminous poetic that he would explore throughout his life, creating a glissement, between poet and other, writer and reader—a poetry of presence and immediacy, intimacy and*

empathic encounter in the purest diction and most "classically austere forms" of any poet of his generation.

"Theater" is the first poem in *On the Motion and Immobility of Douve*. The figure of Douve is based on a young girl he knew who died a sudden and tragic death. The poems in the book alternate between poetic quatrains and prose paragraphs, and between the image of the dead young woman and death in general. As the sequence progresses, the speaker seeks to discover his own destiny as he identifies with the words of the young woman. The speaker says, "Douve je parle en toi" (Douve, I speak in you):

> And though great cold rises in your being,
> However burning the frost of our intimacy
> Douve, I speak in you; and I enshroud you
> In the act of knowing and of naming

where the act of naming and of knowing restores her presence. Eventually, he realizes that the proper form of mourning for the dead young woman is silence, as it is for his own eventual transformation and death. For an alternate translation of this strange and difficult piece, and of the whole book, see Galway Kinnell's *On the Motion and Immobility of Douve* (Bloodaxe Books Ltd, 1997).

Song: Pervigilium Veneris (Anonymous)

Spring, & the goddess, a clear sound from the waves;
& in the groves & hollows, the mating rains,
& in the small houses of the leaves:

Let whoever who has not loved, love tomorrow,
Whoever has loved, love tomorrow

& the blood rising & the ocean foam,
Horses & sand, violence of horses
When the goddess arrives, wave-born in the mating rain:

Let all who have not loved, love tomorrow,
& all who have loved, love tomorrow

For the year's been like death; & now there are flowers.
For the year's been still & gray; & now there is wind.
How the dew is scattered & the night wind calls,
How the tears about to fall
Are held, & the blush begins.
Now the stars rain down on cloudless nights,
& the stiff gestures of married women grow soft.
The rose is wed to the dew, & the pale dresses
Of flowers open softly at morning, to ocean gems
& flames, & to the purple of first light,
Past responsibilities, past care, all
But Love's kisses & the rising blood:

Let any who have not loved, love tomorrow,
& any who have loved, love tomorrow.

Now the young girl approaches her father
That his strictness might waver.
& the young man at the front door does not hesitate,

& in the grove, the chorus sings,
& in the field there is constant song.

Let whoever has not loved, love tomorrow
& whoever has loved, love tomorrow

& the goddess rules & gives commands,
That the flower shall be spent in the forest,
That no wild thing come forth but shall be loved,
& the women seek their lovers, in her honor;
Listen, for the swans grow hoarse in the streams,
& the animals are gentle, with gentle songs.
The birds break their winter silence, & the rains begin.

Yet there is one song a young girl sings.
& sings so beautifully,
That love seems the reason, not sorrow...
So the tradesman stops in the forest, & is silent,
& puts down his tools, & is silent;
& listens as she sings so beautifully
To no one & to everyone,
When shall my own spring come,
& my silence end?

Let whoever has not loved, love tomorrow
& whoever has loved, love tomorrow.

Free Union (Andre Breton)

My wife with the wood-burning hair
Whose thoughts are summer lightning
Whose waist is the size of an hourglass
Like an otter in the teeth of a tiger
My wife with the mouth of cockade-ribbons
And a bouquet of brightest stars
Whose teeth are the footprints of a white mouse on snow
Whose tongue is amber and polished glass
My wife whose tongue is a stabbed wafer
The tongue of a doll that opens and closes its eyes
With an incredible stone language
My wife whose eyelashes are stick-figures drawn by children
Whose eyebrows are the nests of swallows
My wife whose temples are the slate color of greenhouse roofs
When the windows are completely fogged-up
My wife with the champagne shoulders
And dolphin head fountains under ice
My wife with match-stick wrists
My wife with fingers of chance and the ace of hearts
With fingers of cut hay
My wife with armpits of marten and beechnut
And St. John's Eve
Of privet and nests of angelfish
With arms of sea foam and river locks
And a mix of wheat and the mill
My wife with the rocket legs
With the movements of clockwork and despair
My wife with the marrow of elder calves
My wife whose feet are initials
Whose feet are key-rings and the feet of drunk steeplejacks
My wife whose neck is unpearled barley
Whose throat is a Valley of Gold
Whose bed-time encounters are torrents

Whose breasts are of the night
My wife whose breasts are molehills under the sea
My wife whose breasts are crucibles of rubies
Are the ghost breasts of roses under dew
My wife whose belly is an unfolding fan of days
Whose belly is a giant claw belly
My wife with the back of a bird fleeing vertically
With a back of quicksilver
At the other side of the light
With a neck of worn stone and wet chalk
And of a broken glass from which we have just drunk
My wife with basket hips
Hips of luster and arrowheads
And the stems of white peacock feathers
And of insensitive scales
My wife with a backside of sandstone and asbestos
My wife with a back of swans
My wife with the buttocks of spring
With the sex of brilliant iris
My wife with the Sex of Place and Platypus
My wife with the sex of seaweed and old-time sweets
My wife of the sex of the mirror
My wife with eyes full of tears
With eyes of a violet panoply and magnetic needles
My wife with savanna eyes
My wife with eyes of water for prisoners
My wife with the eyes of forests falling under the ax
My wife with eyes that are the level equal of earth and water and fire.

Elsa At The Mirror (Louis Aragon)

In the very middle of our tragedy
Seated at her mirror on that long day
She combed her golden hair and I seemed to see
Her patient hands quench a great fire
There in the very middle of our tragedy

And during that long day at her mirror
As she combed her golden hair it seemed to me
That it was as if she played on a harp but as one
Who did not believe in the melody even a little
All during that long day seated at her mirror

And as she combed her golden hair it seemed to me
That she martyred an old memory with pleasure
Seated at her mirror during that long day
Reviving spent flowers of old fires endlessly
But never speaking of it as another might have

She martyred an old memory with pleasure
There in the very middle of our tragedy
And the world resembled that cursed mirror
And the comb parted fires of silken treasure
And those fires lit the corners of old memory

It was in the very middle of our tragedy
As a Thursday is in the middle of the week

And during a long day seated in this memory
She saw distantly in her mirror one after another

The death of the great actors of our tragedy
Names so well known that I don't have to say them

They who were the best in this cursed world

And see how her hair turns to gold as she sits

Through these long evenings of the flames
Silently combing out the reflections of the fire.

Theater (Yves Bonnefoy)

I

I saw you running on terraces,
Fighting the wind,
The cold bleeding on your lips.

And I saw you break up and rejoice at being dead
O more beautiful than lightning
When it stains the white windows of your blood.

II

The dying summer gave you a monotonous pleasure, as we despise the imperfect drunkenness of living,

"Rather the ivy," did you say, "is the attachment of ivy to the stones of its night: of a presence without exit, a face without root.

"Last happy window torn by the solar nail, rather in the mountains this village in which to die.

"Rather that wind ..."

III

It was a wind stronger than our memories,
Stupor of dresses and cries of rocks—and you passed in front of these
    flames
Gridded head split hands and all
Seeking death on the ecstatic drumbeats of your actions.

It was the day of your breasts
And you reigned at last absent from my head.

IV

I wake, it's raining. The wind penetrates you, Douve, the moor of pines asleep near me. I'm on a terrace, in a death hole. They shake, these large dogs made entirely of leaves.

The arm you lift, suddenly, on a door, illuminates me through ages. Village of embers, every moment I see you born, Douve.

Every moment die.

V

The arm that is lifted and the arm that is turned at the same moment
Are only for our heads that have grown heavy and dull,
But in rejecting these sheets of greenery and mud
There remains only the one fire of the kingdom of death.

The leg released from the war where the high wind penetrates
Driving the heads of rain before him
Will light you only to the threshold of this kingdom,
Gestures of Douve, gestures already slower, black gestures.

VI

What pallor overcomes you, underground river, what artery breaks in
you, where the echo resounds from your fall?

That arm that you raise suddenly opens, ignites. Your face recedes.
What growing mist tears your eyes away? Slow cliff of shadow, border of
death.

Silent arms welcome you, trees from another shore.

VII

Hurt and confused in the leaves,
But taken by the blood of lost tracks,
Accomplice yet again of living.

I saw you at the end of your struggle
Hesitate on the borders of silence and water,
And the dirty mouth of the last stars,
And break with a cry at the horror of watching in the night.

O standing in the air suddenly hard as a rock
A beautiful gesture of coal.

VIII

The crazy music starts in the hands, the knees, then it's the head that
crackles, the music asserts itself under the lips, his certainty penetrates the
underground slope of the face.

Now the carpentry is broken up. Now we proceed to the tearing out of
sight.

IX

White under a ceiling of insects, poorly lit, in profile
And your robe stained by the venom of the lamps,
I find you,
Your mouth higher than a river breaking in the distance on the earth.

To be defeated and then gathered by the invincible being,
A presence re-entering the torch of the cold,
O watchman always I find you dead,
Douve saying Phoenix I watch in this cold.

X

    I see Douve stretched out. A rustling at the highest point of the carnal space. The black princes rush their mandibles into this space where the hands of Douve develop, her bones defeated by their mutating flesh in a gray cloth lit by the massive spider.

XI

Covered with the silent humus of the world,
Through the rays of a living spider,
Subject to the changing of the sand
Cut to pierces by secret knowledge.

Ready for a party in a vacuum
For teeth bared as for love,

Fountain of my death, before me, unbearable.

XII

    I see Douve stretched out. In the scarlet city of the air, where the branches fight across her face, where roots find their way into her body— she radiates a strident joy as of insects, a terrible music.

    At the black step of the earth, ravaged, exultant Douve joins the lamp of the gnarled plateaus.

XIII
Your face tonight lit by the earth,
But I see your eyes become corrupt
Until the word face becomes meaningless.

Here is an image:
An interior sea lit by rotating eagles.
I hold you to a cold depth where the pictures become impossible.

XIV
     I see Douve stretched out. In a white room, eyes surrounded by plaster, dizzy mouth and hands doomed to lush grass that invades from all sides.

     The door opens. An orchestra moves forward. And the faceted eyes, fluffy thorax, cold heads with beaks, and mandibles, flood everything.

XV
O endowed with a profile where the earth persists,
I see you disappear.

Bare grass on your lips and luster of flint
Invent your last smile,

Deep science where
The old cerebral bestiary
Burns to ash.

XVI
     Keep the dark fire where our slopes converge! Under these vaults I see you shine, motionless and moaning, caught in the vertical net of death.

     Masterful, overturned, at sunsets in funereal space, she slowly moves lower.

XVII
The ravine enters your mouth now,
The five fingers are scattered among the hazards of the forest,

Your head sinks between the grasses now,
The gorge blazes with snow and wolves,
The eyes light on which of these are the passengers of death and it is
    we in this wind in this water in this cold now.

XVIII
    Exact presence that no flame restrains; bearer of secret cold; alive,
blood reborn and growing where the poem is torn,

    It was necessary for you to appear at the deaf limits, that you undergo
the test of this funeral site where your light lessens.

    O more beautiful with death in your laughter! I dare to meet you now,
I support the brilliance of your actions.

XIX
At the first day of cold our head escapes
Like a prisoner fleeing into higher air,
But Douve in this instant the arrow fails
The crown of palms is broken from its head.

So we thought we would reincarnate our gestures,
But the head denied it like a drink of cold water,
And death smiles in the bunting of your smile,
Tempting a last opening into the thickness of the world.

Felicia Zamora

If starlight be

If starlight be how visible & electromagnetic your form; & all the parts of the unseen we take for granted; decisions on Capitol Hill spoken into law without say of anyone other than, say *elected official,* say *O radiation of you lost behind another broken system;* say *we made it someone's job to speak for us & now & now;* what light bares in us.

᳐

If starlight be waves in carry through space; say *speed of light in a vacuum;* how a country moves with the voices of its people on its back; how we carried by misdeeds in a justice system that sees color & distastes it, sees the poor under its gavel & wields despite, blindfold long removed moons ago, scales in twist in distort.

If starlight be how you produce, charged particle, in acceleration; wave of you brings energy & momentum to give from a source to matter you interact with; how generous a source found in lungs, brain, & aortic sack; say *what makes you human makes you powerful;* let all who treat you inhumane feel your energy in pulse.

෴

If starlight be & you single photon rest in mass of zero, rest in the infinite design of a mouth open before all the numbers in the universe tumble out & become yours for the taking; linger brief, here, on the verge; do not let roles & officials wipe your name, use your trachea, your tongue to speak, lest you begin to forget.

∾

ABOUT FELICIA ZAMORA

Felicia Zamora is the author of the books *Of Form & Gather*, winner of the 2016 Andrés Montoya Poetry Prize (University of Notre Dame Press 2017), *& in Open, Marvel* (Parlor Press 2017), and *Instrument of Gaps* (Slope Editions 2018). *Of Form &*  *Gather* was listed as one of the "9 Outstanding Latino Books Recently Published by Independent and University Presses" by NBC News. She won the 2015 Tomaž Šalamun Prize from *Verse*, authored two chapbooks, and was the 2017 Poet Laureate for Fort Collins, CO. Her published works may be found or forthcoming in *Alaska Quarterly Review, Crazyhorse, Indiana Review, jubilat, North American Review, OmniVerse, Poetry Daily, Poetry Northwest, Prairie Schooner, Sugar House Review, The Cincinnati Review, The Georgia Review, TriQuarterly Review, Tupelo Quarterly, Verse Daily, West Branch,* and others. She holds an MFA from Colorado State University, is the Associate Poetry Editor for the *Colorado Review* and is the Education Programs Coordinator for the Virginia G. Piper Center for Creative Writing at Arizona State University.

ABOUT THE POEM

"If starlight be" belongs to a larger manuscript entitled, *Body of Render,* which wonders about internal and external impacts on our humanity due to political and societal decisions on a national level that strip away basic human rights. What does it mean to be an underrepresented population in this country where the most powerful seat in the land unashamedly perpetuates racist, misogynistic, homophobic, and classist behaviors? How do we, as human beings, move toward love and healing, in the context of broken systems? How do we look to starlight, to illuminate our bones, our cells, our failed structures, our past—to better understand ourselves and our necessary future where all people may live without oppression and persecution. This poem wants to give voice to the voiceless, to pull back the charade of systems that keep us oppressed, to show the power of the human life, to tell those who treat others inhumanly: *enough; not anymore.*

Chet'la Sebree

Tumor Response

At North Star Grill, Aunt Gi and I order
most of the appetizers on the menu: rockfish bites,
a pound of steamed shrimp, lemon-pepper hot wings.
Over this feast, I see her cry for the first time
about the glioblastoma, the shifting of brain tissue
that only extends her life by months. She murmurs
something about hair loss. And I search for things to say—
wishing her sentence was to be breast-less or barren.

It's gonna be alright, she whispers, recomposing.
Careful, hands dusted in Old Bay, as she wipes
what we're both digesting from her face.
Will you take me to the water, she asks as she returns
to peeling the carapace off a shrimp's body
exposing its pink flesh.

Survivor's Guilt as Steven-Johnson's Syndrome

Phyllo epidermis turns dandruff
after strawberry skin—
pockmarked by pore and follicle—
after the body boils to blister, but before
doctors slow the spread with steroids.
I wake each day a new person—
my yesterday's snake skin sloughed off.
I dry my remnants in the closet,
wait for my molten selves to dry to dust.

Years later air-filled blisters form
on my fingertips, lyse leaving me liminal
between past and present selves, shells.
My fingerprint unrecognizable
until my transformation is complete—
new skin tender as wet wings
of butterfly exiting chrysalis.

Anxiety

Six days of dishes
by the sink (dried

white of creamed soup,
wilted salad) produces

the same sensation
as heart burn or

swallowed smoke—
branches of fire

Mylanta might stoke.
There's Benedryl by the bed,

hydroxyzine in the cabinet—

from the time
my body brailed,
cheeks cherubed—

I've hidden from myself.
I don't know
my HIV status

or my credit score, but
I know this

is a poem:
a poem is a poem is a chance

to pretend I know what I'm doing,
that I know the outcome—

a body buttoned into a bodice of lace.

ABOUT CHET'LA SEBREE

Chet'la Sebree was the 2014-2016 Stadler Fellow at Bucknell University's Stadler Center for Poetry. She holds an MFA from American University and has received fellowships from The MacDowell Colony, Yaddo, Hedgebrook, and Vermont Studio Center. Her work has recently appeared or is forthcoming in *Kenyon Review, Crazyhorse, Pleiades, Guernica,* and *Gulf Coast.*

ABOUT THE POEMS

A few weeks after I finished my MFA, my aunt was diagnosed with terminal brain cancer; she was like a second mother to me. In the midst of her illness and my grief, I wrote poems to try to make sense of what was happening. For me, poetry is a way of ordering the chaos, a way of slowing down the world into digestible chucks. Of course, no sense could really be made of anything except of my emotions. For me, these poems were a way to confront the reality of losing her.

Although only "Tumor Response" is a sonnet, many of the poems in this series started as fourteen-liners. The formal constraint of the sonnet structure—specifically the Petrarchan octave and sestet—put pressure on the language. The tight structures forced me to grapple with illness and loss head-on. Although many of the poems found lives of their own outside of the sonnet, the remnants persist: the problem, the volta, the push toward resolution.

Poetry Journal

Early Morning Riding The Bus....
May 1, 2018

Blind fingers & toes, blind face

Arms, legs, torso—

Woman opposite

Sizing me up

Like something

In a market

Blind cabbage

& me thinking

How fair

She once

Must have been

A Victorian doll

Poems sticking from my pockets

Some about sea horses

Some about manners of love

Wintering

April 20, 2018
—in memory of Jarkko Laine

Memory loves coffee

And steam pipes

Banging inside the walls

O what have you.

On Helsinki's esplanade

We walked

In matching trench coats—

Two Bogarts with poems

Sticking from our pockets.

Some about sea horses

Some about manners of love

Some about snowstorms burying books.

Disability, Resurrection, Poetry
April 1, 2018

It's Easter Sunday and I'm thinking about human equality, disability, and the poetry uniting both. Strange really, the resurrection of Christ, equal rights, a poetics. Here's what I mean: Christ rises from his grave, the very action the most extraordinary figure of rehabilitation in human history. All resurrection myths proclaim equality is not out of reach—that soon enough you'll be unrecognizable to yourself, clean, bright, and favored like others.

Poetry may not always be concerned with religion or equality. The early modernist poets in their desire to rival the immediacy of photographs were at times dispassionate—see Imagism or Vorticism as practiced by Pound—yet poetry often is where we find empathy. I wept alone in my faculty office one afternoon when, after a day of pain, my legally blind eyes unable to keep up with the tasks before me, in the days before reliable speech technology, I read the following poem by Adrienne Rich with my left eye only a half inch from the page:

I know you are reading this poem
late, before leaving your office
of the one intense yellow lamp-spot and the darkening window
in the lassitude of a building faded to quiet
long after rush-hour. I know you are reading this poem
standing up in a bookstore far from the ocean
on a grey day of early spring, faint flakes driven
across the plains' enormous spaces around you.
I know you are reading this poem
in a room where too much has happened for you to bear
where the bedclothes lie in stagnant coils on the bed
and the open valise speaks of flight
but you cannot leave yet. I know you are reading this poem
as the underground train loses momentum and before running
up the stairs
toward a new kind of love
your life has never allowed.
I know you are reading this poem by the light
of the television screen where soundless images jerk and slide
while you wait for the newscast from the intifada.

I know you are reading this poem in a waiting-room
of eyes met and unmeeting, of identity with strangers.
I know you are reading this poem by fluorescent light
in the boredom and fatigue of the young who are counted out,
count themselves out, at too early an age. I know
you are reading this poem through your failing sight, the thick
lens enlarging these letters beyond all meaning yet you read on
because even the alphabet is precious.
I know you are reading this poem as you pace beside the stove
warming milk, a crying child on your shoulder, a book in your
hand
because life is short and you too are thirsty.
I know you are reading this poem which is not in your
    language
guessing at some words while others keep you reading
and I want to know which words they are.
I know you are reading this poem listening for something, torn
between bitterness and hope
turning back once again to the task you cannot refuse.
I know you are reading this poem because there is nothing else
left to read
there where you have landed, stripped as you are.
–Adrienne Rich, from *An Atlas of the Difficult World*

Consider a "stripped" reader—consider her bent low. Stripped is vulnerability, a nakedness, and yet it's also the first turn toward new language, one that allows us to tenderly imagine ourselves renewed.

It's renewal that interests me. If equality is a moral concept, as I believe it is, than the broken body is also a moral agent; if "where you have landed" is neither a sacred or profane space, it is solely Jeffersonian—embodiment, whatever the circumstance is human, therefore fully, entirely human. In Disability Studies we often speak of resisting "overcoming narratives" by which we mean a resistance to medical persuasion—the idea that humans are only valuable insofar as they can be cured of their maladies. We call this the "medical model" of disability and many a disabled person has written a book touting his or her "miracle cure" often attributing it to a marriage of god and science. Sometimes of course it's god alone or simply science. In either case the subtext of these books is routine: only a physically able and firm body has value. I think such stories are immoral for unlike Adrienne Rich's poem which holds out the possibility of new directions in despair, overcoming narratives are steadfast in their insistence only the healthy body matters.

In his new book "One Another's Equals" Jeremy Waldron observes:

> "When we talk about equality, one of the most important distinctions we have to make is between prescriptive and descriptive equality. Descriptive statements tell us how things are, and prescriptive statements tell us how things ought to be and / or what things ought to be done. Crudely, we can say descriptively (or deny descriptively) that people are equal in some respect; we can say their opportunities are equal or that there used to be less inequality of income than there is now. Or we can say, prescriptively, that people ought to be equal. We can say that in general—for example, that they ought to be treated with equal respect—or we can say it in some particular regard, such as their income or opportunities."

Excerpt From: Jeremy Waldron. "One Another's Equals." iBooks.
He adds:

> *"Prescriptive statements call for something to be done that might not otherwise be done."*

This is essentially what poetry is or concerns itself with. And one thinks of Robert Kennedy's famous declaration: "There are those that look at things the way they are, and ask why? I dream of things that never were, and ask why not?"

Resurrection is prescriptive and whether its a fantasy or not matters less to me than its moral inference: we are equal in renewal which differs profoundly from being cured or healed. Jesus, risen, still had his wounds. He remains, even glorified, our physical equal, in flesh our aspirational moral equal.

The best disability poetry tends to work in these areas though it may not be overtly spiritual in nature. Embracing the equal status of the disabled body is invariably renewing.

In her poem "Future Biometrics" Jillian Weise writes:

the body that used to
contain your daughter

we found it
behind the fence

It was in a red coat
It was collected

Is she saved
Is she in the system

You're lucky
we have other bodies

to put your daughter in
Come on down

to the station

Weise combines the medical model, the curative, with a post-human vision of cyber-resurrection. The "it" daughter, not entirely human, dead behind a fence will be transmogrified through technological means, industrial means, one imagines a whole new shipment of alternative bodies arriving by train. A motto for the poem could read: "beware what resurrection you're calling for" or the like.

Jim Ferris describes resurrection as survival—after eugenics, after Aristotle, the disabled actually dare to thrive:

"Tell Aristotle"
As to the exposure and rearing of children, let there be a law that no deformed child shall live. —Aristotle, Politics

Tell Aristotle I lived.
    Tell him Dave did too.
Tell him the state has not
    yet fallen, though you know
kids these days. Tell him perhaps
    all our words are but
elaborations, repetitions
    of that crier's claim.
Tell Aristotle, tell the Spartans,

tell the legions of those
who think they can't afford the difference
    that difference makes,
tell Montaigne, tell Hobbes,
    tell Dr. Tiergarten
and that off-key singer
    of sad and silly songs,
tell them the useless eaters
    have survived,
tell them there are more of us now
    than ever, disorderly,
imperfect, splashing out the gene pool,
    what a messy species,
tell them my brother Dave and I
    inhabit this moment,
tell Aristotle we are alive,
    tell them all we thrive.

Resurrection is imperfect, splashing out of the gene pool, more of us now, and implicitly, firmly, prescriptively, morally equal.
The poet Laurie Clements Lambeth writes:

and then there are days when I can stride across the house
five times even, springing forward with an armful of laundry

as though I never forgot how, no longer offering the body
instruction in hip tuck or the proper undulation of each foot

(hold wall, heel first, steady now, lift the next). My gratitude
at such moments is not for the walking, that easy

grace. It's for the shadow, that other gait hovering around
my frame, a faint, wavering outline, staggering dragged

water-edge purling behind. How can one measure time or
space?
The miles I saw stretch across this little house unfurled a span

to heave through, now condensed to mere feet. I will see those miles again, I know, and somehow now: I keep a foot in each world.

Embodied, prescriptive, we're equally unknowable—the truest definition of equivalence and equality one may ever know. Disability as poetics, an epistemology is a resurrectionist school but not a school of overcoming or cure.

From a Birthday Notebook...

March 29, 2018

Happy Birthday Stephen—

Sitting alone with Thelonious Monk

Aged fifteen

Solo in the attic

With a radio…

**

The Finnish poet Jarkko Laine once told me he lived on Deep Ditch
Road.

The Egyptologist on the subway told me about mummified beetles in
tiny sarcophagi.

**

Now and then I recall a certain turtle.

^^

Happy birthday.

The fence will not be fully repaired.

I fear my teeth have more wisdom than my hands.

This is also my Finnish grandmother's birthday.

She was a devout Lutheran and therefore not much fun.

She did however send me photos of herself, not having much fun.

**

Just this morning, for a time, I became Heraclitus, the dark one, then,
just as sudden, I was my father who when young imagined he would be a
writer before World War II changed him, made him somber, until he
believed literature was a childish thing. He's gone now. The poems he
loved are still on my bookshelf. I admit I try to read them as he did—
mindful of another's joy and curiosity and yes, apprehension.

**

On his birthday—I'm not sure which one—Heraclitus invented the
string clock….

Jordan Smith

America, a Trance

Don't think this is over.
The fiddler's got another hundred trips through
Goin' to That Free State left in his bow arm

And another dozen anecdotes about how it doesn't mean
What you think it does.
It sounds like it's about freedom. It's about memory,
And those unforgivable injuries, taxes and rents.

Thoreau's master surveyor whacked the boy with a switch
So he'd never forget the boundary corner.

The fiddler's got one squint eye
And the kind of seriousness you don't find much anymore
Until you do, and it's too late;
He's into a set of cross-A tunes that might end Sunday
If it ends at all.

See, you're learning it his way:
Sitting by the wood stove, sweating, bow a little slack,
Gut strings and nothing written down.
If there's a dog at your feet, a glass by your hand,

You earned it, you'll keep it, playing the same damn tune.

Lorca's Mercedes

Black, of course.
Even the numerals on the license, the charcoal-numbered gauges.

He has purloined it from the mayor, that unregenerate Falangist,
The one who decreed the end of measure.

How modern, the words on the proclamations.
They are a taste in his mouth, rubber streaked on asphalt.

The cheap black tobacco one worker offers another.
Is his small blessing.

What hero publishes the account of his descent, grudging,
What sort of man attends a funeral to count the flowers in the wreaths?

He cannot tell the olive grove from the alley's black end.
It is all one to him.

The precision of the pistons in their dark oil,
Deep in the cavern of the engine, there are steps he can count.

ABOUT JORDAN SMITH

Jordan Smith is the author of seven books of poems, most recently *Clare's Empire*, a fantasia on the life and work of John Clare from The Hydroelectric Press, and *The Light in the Film*, *The Names of Things Are Leaving*, and *For Appearances*,  all from the University of Tampa Press. His earlier books appeared from Princeton University Press, Wesleyan University Press, and Copper Beech Press, and his chapbooks are from The Pudding Press, Right Hand Pointing, and Swan Scythe. With his wife, Malie, he lives in upstate New York, where he is the Edward Everett Hale Jr., Professor of English at Union College. His work has been strongly influenced by the visual arts, and especially by his association with Walter Hatke, whose paintings appear on two of his book covers and with whom he is completing a limited edition of broadsides.

ABOUT THE POEMS

"America, A Trance" and "Lorca's Mercedes"

My friend, Ed Pavlic, sent me his poem, "Don't Ask: A Questionnaire," where he quoted a phrase connecting America and trance, and that got me thinking about the experience of playing old-time music, with its trance-like repetitions and complicated history, and a tune I was learning, "Gone to That Free State," by John Ashby and The Free State Ramblers, where according to the recording notes "free state" referred to the refusal to pay taxes and rent. That seemed right in line with my long-time interest in trying to reach back into the past without sentimentalizing it, or at least without ignoring the violence that's connected with ideas of freedom.

At about the same time, I was reading Sarah Arvio's new translations of Lorca, as fine a poet of the connections between tradition, bloodshed, and the uncanniness of the archaic as you can find, and somehow the juxtaposition of Lorca and a black Mercedes (that ultimate combination of modern design and 1930s fascism) got stuck in my mind. I wanted to see where it would take me, with the landscape of Lorca's poems as a guide.

Ron Drummond

Blood Red

As if blood comes in one color.

You think of your friend's last moments, his breath imperceptible.

The hapless novice hospice worker:

> *He's gone*   *Oh not yet*   *Now*   *I think*   *Oh no*

until the stethoscope, the mirror, the feather all confirm his passing.

You caress your friend's cheek and from between his lips pours blood
long-pooled from a tongue he must have bitten maybe hours before,

blood the blackest red you've ever seen,

as if garnet had wrestled mahogany and mahogany had won,

as if maroon had closed its eyes forever.

How does a survivor survive such a red?

A mentor's curandera urged you: *¡Lárgate de ese cuarto!*

Ha!   Easier said than done!

To *get out of that room*, even if *that room* is in your mind, you need a door.

A decade of failing doors later, consider this:

For your friend who wore the same green bomber jacket everywhere
and whose moustache hailed from another era,

re-purpose that beef-liver-at-midnight red through the gift of a bit of
drag.

Imagine those ten limber theatre-bibliographer fingers of his

and lacquer their nails one by one with that deepest of reds.

For each nail the lacquer shall remain the same hue, but the name will
change.

You shall paint his thumbnail *Stump Hollow Red*
because leaving town to care for his mom was never a winter-break
waste.

His index-finger nail: *Scratch 'n Sniff Red*
as in "*Polyester*'s not *Polyester* without a scratch 'n sniff card."

His middle-finger nail: *Mamet Miller Red*.
"*Glengarry Glen Ross? Death of a Fucking Salesman.*"

The nail on his ringless ring finger: *Johanna Red*
for his begging Sondheim not to cut a single reprise from *Sweeney*.

And his pinky nail: *Little Foxes Red*.
"No apartment's tiny if it grants you a glimpse of Miss Taylor's arrival
for her Broadway debut."

Now paint the nails on his other hand:

Audience Extra Red
Queens College Red The One That Got Away Red
Becco Red   Laugh Out Loud Red.

But leave his toes alone.

ABOUT RON DRUMMOND

Ron Drummond is the author of *Why I Kick At Night* (Portlandia Press) and is currently translating Jacobo Fijman's *Molino Rojo*. His poetry appears in the Penguin textbook *Literature as Meaning* and in the anthologies *Poetry Nation, Poetry After 9/11, This New Breed, Saints of Hysteria* and *Flicker and Spark*. His poems and translations have been published in the literary journals *Assaracus, Barrow Street, Bellevue Literary Review, Borderlands, Columbia Review, Court Green, Global City Review, Guernica, The Journal, Northwest Review, Ocean State Review, Terra Incognita* and *U.S. Latino Review*. He has been awarded fellowships from Ragdale, VCCA, Blue Mountain Center, and the Macondo Foundation.

ABOUT THE POEM

This poem was born in part out of my impatience while reading the works of a naturalist who was, to my taste, over-fond of the phrase "wine red." This impatience led to scribbling of my own that amounted to an ungenerous rant on what I perceived as that gentleman's vagueness (fueled by my less than confident certainty that burgundy and claret have different hues). The place that I did not expect my cocky pencil to take me to was a Times Square studio apartment with a red in it that I had avoided speaking about, let alone writing on, for over ten years – a very specific red of a very specific moment. Once I was facing that red fully, it took over, and my prior complaint vanished from the poem. The new beginning became "As if blood comes in one color." I took on the second person voice to both protect myself and propel myself, to distance and invite. The poem was written as a door for myself and as a door for the reader. I chose to re-purpose the red of the title in the ritual/spell that is the second half of the poem, and to open up the poem through the progressive revelation of a particular biography and voice, and perhaps, a spirit.

Martin Willitts Jr

Counting Cows While Waiting for Rain

rain ends at the edge of the blindside
where the fence divides the familiar
from the world asleep

cows thread through the same path
browned and flattened by their passing

all around the burnt sienna dust rises
when there is not enough rain
scattering like a few letters home
saying they are alright in the city
where hopes can go dry overnight

what in this life can save us

the temporary rain is waning
the grass chewed to the nub
and although we have a hammer and nail
we cannot fix what is wrong in this world

ABOUT MARTIN WILLITTS, JR.

Martin Willitts Jr is a retired Librarian living in Syracuse, NY. He was nominated for 15 Pushcarts and 12 Best of the Net awards. He is the winner of 2013 Bill Holm Witness Poetry Contest; 2014 Broadsided award; 2014 Dylan Thomas International Poetry Award; and, Rattle Ekphrastic Challenge, June 2015, Editor's Choice. He has over 20 chapbooks, plus 11 full-length collections including *How to Be Silent* (FutureCycle Press, 2016). He won the National Ecological Poetry Award for his full-length collection *Searching For*  *What You Cannot See* (Hireath Press, 2013). His poems have appeared in *Blue Fifth Review, About Place, Kentucky Review, Perfume River Review, Bitter Oleander, Tipton Poetry Review, Nine Mile Magazine, Comstock Review, Centrifugal Eye, Stone Canoe*, and others. His full-length collection, *Dylan Thomas and the Writing Shed* about his visit to Wales, is forthcoming to FutureCycle Press in 2017.

He won the 2016 Individual Artist Grant from CNYArts, funded by the New York State Council of the Arts, for his countywide "Poetry on the Bus" program, selecting 48 poems about the theme of "Tolerance", including ages 10-80, all races, and immigrants writing in their native language. This project is being forwarded as an example of literacy and social awareness on a national level. In my picture, I am holding one of the winning poems to show the size of the poetry display found in many local (CENTRO) buses.

ABOUT THE POEM

"Counting Cows While Waiting for Rain". Every summer from the ages 5-17, I worked on my grandparent's Mennonite-Amish farm. This meant hard work with hard lessons, using old-time equipment, hand plows, no electricity, three-hole outhouses, and community building of houses and barns. I learned blacksmithing, how to slaughter animals when I was five, how to make change at a roadside stand and give more than a dozen for the price of a dozen, how to plant in rain or beating sun, and how to shoe a horse. I learned geometry before I went to school by using a gravity-fed saw, how to pluck a chicken without getting feathers anywhere, how to predict weather by watching five different kinds of animals. In this poem, I am thinking of my father who left the Mennonite-Amish ways to go to the city, yet he wanted me to experience these old ways. I still remember how to blacksmith and make a weathervane, or how to build a house without nails. Currently, I am using less and less punctuation. I am trying to trust my use of line and stanza breaks to get away from punctuation. I still have not broken the habit of comas, periods, and long EM dashes.

Other Engines

.

Introduction

Steve Kuusisto

I don't remember who said it but other engines power American poetry which is a fancy way of asserting our poetry's capaciousness and daring. Poets from Russia and Chile have found a home in our national literature. While English departments were talking almost exclusively of Eliot and Stevens, Gwendolyn Brooks was writing arguably the best poetry in the United States. We are now seeing a poetry and poetics charged by the neurodiversity movement and experiencing a growing awareness that autist writers and those who are "on the spectrum" as laypersons like to call neurological differences, are writing some of the most original and inventive poetry of our time.

This comes as no surprise to me for I'm a disabled poet who's traveled in the many circles of disability arts. Certainly over the past twenty years I've been lucky to meet extraordinary poets, painters, dancers, photographers, actors who happen to have disabilities and have turned embodied difference into richly creative epistemologies. Moreover I've been lucky to know two of the poets in this festschrift who are both nonspeaking writers. One may say their words come from a great distance to reach the page. Yes. But what I find so remarkable is that in poem after poem our readers will see here there's a commingling of tenderness, clarity, outrage, Dickins' "telling it slant"—vitalities, appetites, cosmic itches, and yes, an overt disregard for niceties. We used to say that poetry was uncooked or "beat" if it spoke without regard for convention. The poems that follow are not raw, they're representative of lives that move fast and which, in poetic terms, have little use for stoves.

Tito Mukhopadhyay

Air

I once saw a picture -
a page from a science journal,
A smog over
a city,

questions or
accusations thrown
perhaps
at the observer.

While raw
piles of pollution was
piling up on
Curd like air, the
population of the town
breathed, drowned,
and then got used to
the smelling
concentration of the sky.
*No one gets to see
the stars anymore!*

Headlights of
cars beamed at
each other
through the twilight
hours of rush.

The background in the picture
Smeared in smoke
measured an incoherent distance,
Inch by inch in depth
the disappearing
city.

A man stood in
front of everything,
on that page,
shaped by the street light
from behind,
Wearing some kind of a
protection mask around
his nose—

'Could be waiting for a bus
'Could be
deeply absorbing thoughts,
absorbing the fumes,
a diver before diving and
disappearing
under the
Smog and vapor -
used to living; adapting

to the grinding existential path of
survival—An
example of human race who needs
to verify his presence of
blood and bones
with his lungs full of
ashes.

Calculations

Right there
sitting on his shadow,
Closer to the sun than you or me,

The Kalahari
staring at him like an aging
ancestor—
Probing his frown,

a Bushman was calculating
the number of times
the clouds came and went by
casting shadows through
him.

When did it
rain last? He remembered how
the rain—
a visitor from the dunes,
would erase the sky
at least once in a
while—brief and fierce
—How the ground flowed
and spilled!

His son - now maybe three
or three and half
approximating with his own
Forehead frowns,
may never see how
things looked under the rain.

He calculated those
mirage moments—when
ostriches used to be plenty,

used to scatter
dusty feathers—How they
ran towards the dunes to bring
the Gods from the Sky.

Mrs. P's House

Mrs. P's empty house, insomniac as an old guard,
Watches the new town grow around its weed filled yard,

While standing on a frozen time, stagnant air behind the cold
Walls - dusty layers under creepers and mould,

While knowing that it would be demolished soon
As the contractors discussed—earlier in June

And listens to the trapped sounds, always too familiar-
Of ghostly footsteps or running rats, it alone can hear,

Then tries to ignore their running about, digging floors
While preserving frozen sounds behind its doors.

Dawn the Sonnet

It dawned on him.
—Dawn the verb,
—Dawn the beginning,
—Dawn, the palate of water colours,
Fresh and out of the box
waiting to get mixed up. . . .
—Dawn the time.

(He might as well write that down,
Lest he forgets....)
in the last strokes of fugitive darkness
—*How a complete Night*
was erased with the
sound of the car's ignition.
Dawn: the eraser!

There Were Shapes

There were shapes, suppressed as sorrow
Mixed with voices and ordinary things,

Shapes as suppressed, sorrows mixed
Ordinary voices and those things

Voices suppressed, things like sorrow
Shapes as ordinary when they mixed

Ordinary sorrow mixed in voices,
Suppressed things out of shape,

Mixed sorrow in ordinary shapes
Voices of things suppressing

Suppressed shape is a thing like sorrow
Voices mixed and ordinary.

Voices from ordinary sorrow
Suppressed—when they mixed with things.

ABOUT TITO MUKHOPADHYAY

My Bio is short. I do write. Many times I write, not out of passion but as a sensory outlet just to engage my inside with my outside. There is a lack of parallax between my outside environment and sensory system. Writing helps to keep the balance. Of course I have a diagnosis but I will ignore mentioning it here. When I write, I like to write as an equal.

So I don't exactly call myself a poet or define myself with a diagnosis. Poetry just happens out of my thoughts —like a stray strand of greenish blue light that hits a window after it rains and lingers around before it turns dark.

ABOUT THE POEMS

My poetry remains elusive until I happen to see - a momentary seeing - perhaps a picture on a magazine showing a city under a blanket of smog. The manic outbreak of man-made spills in air heading towards some self inflicting wound perhaps made my poem 'Air' happen. A photograph can warn - and everyone keeps warning each other continuing to make the same mistakes. Mine was just a poetry - not even a warning!

I saw an article once about the Kalahari and entered the brain of a Bushman. Life gets tougher with vanishing of animals; expanding desert; and his holding on to the stoic stubbornness of the relentless challenges - perhaps remembering the number of times he witnessed rain. What holds him back from joining the civilized world - where life is about calculating salary, expenses, taxes, home mortgage, college loans, time to catch a flight or airline delays?

Mrs. P could have sold her house and the house could have inherited a sensory system but has no power to act. If one can imagine, can sense or can understand but cannot exactly protest or defend oneself - one would be like 'Mrs. P's house'.

'Dawn the sonnet' happens to many of us when an early morning neighborhood car drives past one's window, and one wakes up. The birds are not quite awake yet. There is just an empty sound that fills up the time. And a sonnet dawns in. The question lingers - Why the sonnet?

'There were Shapes' - was one of my word games. I thought why not include a game in the process of submission. It sounded something like a poetry. What sounds like a poetry should be a poetry.

Anand Prahlad

Creation

1.
I would keep her company
       when daddy was never home
and the purple value of damson rose
       like flames, burning across acres
of orchards and gardens,
       when the blues gave way to gospels,
gold robes behind the pulpit
       swaying reeds of Bethany
baptist and the black dancing
       scream torn from a sinner's
throat. I would be the tear drop
       of the blessed savior
as she lightly rubbed her palms
       across the thin membrane
of belly skin, slowly up and down
       imparting need to supple bone
tissue, forgiving organs, cells
       blossoming like magnolias
and I would shift in water
       to the touch of singing, weep
the melody of longing, become
       an opal thud, thing pushing.

2.
But when I came I came like the Lord's fury,
       like one of the Lord's biblical plagues.
I came like the wind upturning rooves.
       I came like the sorrow of lost worlds.
I came with one arm missing
       and a bird singing in my pubic bone

and a cavern in my baby bald nest.
            And like a storm I flung them across the room
and pinned them against the banister and walls.
            I covered the house with rain that rose
like fog, with light their bitterness couldn't touch,
            their hatefulness, shame and embarrassment.
Day after day as they seldom fed me, hardly
            changed me or picked me up. Night after night
as they sat spellbound in black and white in front
            of the television, while I grew gills to breath
beneath the surface of my aloneness, fins
            to swim into the currents and depths of plant
breaths, and slowly turned the house into a sea
            where I could feed on chlorophyll, to take
the edges off my hunger, still, I nearly starved.

my shadow's inflection

the lost shadow covered itself
        with my body
                which covered itself with leaves
but still could not evade
        the hideous heels of laughter
            that rained at recess
                on the playground.

it drowned in the wetness
        of the earth
            until there was no breath left
not even for the EM drivers
        with their pretty blue uniforms
           who never showed up anyway
              to frantically resurrect me.

it bent like a hanged effigy,
        a miming ballet dancer
           suspended by orchestra strings.
an actor mimicking tragedy,
        a surrendered devotee in bliss,
           suffused in afternoon sunlight
             and spread across the wall

in the back corner
        of the classroom.
           it multiplied and spasmed
in the needled saffron light,
        bolted from beneath my buttons
           like a jittery farm cat
             and cowered beneath desks and tables.

it was all blue vibrating
        deaf crackling of a burning
           bush, and in the center

a figure

                not suffocating in smoke,

                       not scorched or singed

                              not burning in the furnace.

it propped itself up at the piano

                and stretched out its arms

                       with the tenderness of dove's feet,

the warmth of dog paws,

                and disappeared into the currents

                     of boogie woogie black keys

                           mahalia jackson sonnets

satin mood indigo supreme

                and jasmine brimmed hats

                     turned upside down

umbrella tones in the rain,

                freed like horses' hooves

                     loosed from wagons,

                            loosed from bits and bridles.

it did not whisper on the daily bus.

                it did not shake.

                     did not break through a window

                            smeared with grease from

someone's forehead.

                could not reach out

                     and touch or capture mama

in a far-flung threaded net.

                could only hunker down inside

                     a cornelian-colored cave

beneath my breaking body

                in a field as snowy as white

                     padded walls, as foggy

                            as soporific idling and turns.

it left my body and danced
                    with the sparrows. with the crows.
                            it left me all alone.
                                      it reached out it's spindly arms
into the zigzag flight
                    into the migratory lanes
                          and the muted tales of butterflies.

Askew

It's funny you call me askew, crooked, oblique,

                lopsided, off-center, cockeyed, twisted, and aslant,

                            when I'm the one who's straight,

when it's me who sees the order,

                the patterns certain as circles in a field of corn

        striations on the wings of moths

                        and the tart lines in linens, glazed

discrepancies in petulant, hurried feet

                        ascending into lost arpeggios, unable

or is it unwilling to revise a single note

                of an apocalyptic melody.

It's me who comes behind you, righting

                            chaos, turning the slashed
skin of ancient

landscapes into orders where birds can rest.

                me, the one without feeling, you say,

                without operable sense, usefulness, understanding.

it's me who sees the shapes in your liquid noise,

the aching figures rising out of the pixels

while you fall under the spells of plot

dialogue, and special effects. it's me

rocking back and forth in a bed on the coast

sounding the fog horn you never listen to

keeping the diary, and watching the waves

wash over the wrecked skeletons of ships

and boats, that land here, year after year

like the alto lifting from a groove of vinyl

a graveyard the needle is stuck on.

A molecule of birch

a molecule
of birch
joined to helium
melded
to whole helix
to tortoise
shell split by
cobalt
into halves
like a brain,
like watts
through wires
at the sanitarium.

a seizing
a branch burning
scent of myself
frying
a cloned protein
mustard gas
and sulfonates
dropped
like napalm
on alien tribes
roaming jungles
of my marrow.

the last time,
sickened,
I dreamed
my soul
was iridescent again
and the linnets
in my lungs
were singing,

and the bees
in my belly
were starting
to make honey
and the water
in my kidneys
was somehow
as if Jesus
had dipped
his hands in it.

but this time
the tumor
dreamed
of putting me
into stasis
to heal me.
it dreamed of
serenading t-cells
like sirens
to cure the disease
of me,
the illness
that was literally
my body,
of eliminating
the flesh
and resurrecting
the voice
and teaching me
how to speak again
as if was I back
in this world,
even if I wasn't.

it was spring
and cherry

blossom pink
stars petaled
into tubes
and my heart
was afloat
in liquid space,
in a galaxy of tears
and cotton
distance
touching my skin
and suddenly
the insistent
beeps of monitors
where I truly lived.
A bird
outside the window.

A plane. A white trail of exhaust in vast blue. A dove's cooing in the
blank spaces between blips. The ceiling fan in the mirror across the
room in which I hadn't seen myself in weeks. Everywhere, I was missing.

2.
                    I walk
                or do I float,
            or do I
        surge,
      or do
    I coarse
  like current
lost in the wrong
 century?
   Do I snake along
     like a river
         through
             a canyon
               or a kilobyte
                   of timid mercy

                    humming through
                        wires and cables?

                Is it really me
            who is
          gazing
        out the
        window
          and seeing bones
        glistening
      like dimes
  and pennies

and strung up
from fire
  escapes
      like chimes
          or church bells

                    or trapped in
                crocus sacks
              in the public
            fountain
        is it me
      hearing them
  flute-like
  whistling
    laments
          and dirges?

and I notice
  I say me
      when I also
          mean the body
              I can feel
                  my hands,
                      but I can

no longer
see them.
I stretch them
out but nothing
but the purest
darkness
hovers
in front of me.
Who is *me?*
The taste
of wild greens
is the sound
of plum
is the smell
of the delta.
In the small
lake
of a stethoscope
I see myself
or do I?
is that me
wiping blood
and ash
from my face
and asking myself,
what have I done,
what have I
let them do
to me
and hearing
the breaking
and the wails
in the cities
of my own
bones,
the rage of tsunamis
into which

my bones move
like fragile
catamarans.

Ponies

Every time I see the moon
I think of you.

I think of your big thighs
that slipped over me
like shadows
on the hillside and raced like
the last gallop
of great plains ponies.

I think of your tongue
walking down the steps
in a rotten
old house
and your fingers
opening up a jar
and finally letting go

the butterflies that
spread their wings like
tattooed webs
and maps of slave
routes across
your ribs and belly
across the hollows and valleys
where the doctors
opened you up.

I think of your shimmy
shake walking
on a button,
one leg shorter
than the other, and
always tilted as if
to hold the dark thread

in its dwelling,
as if to keep too much
light from
trickling out

and your amaranth
gurgle of sweat
and bush as wild as
cat's claw
and the stranger
you let loose in me
to mutiny, weep,
to kneel and pray
and to flee into the city

of skin in which
meaning goes on
beyond uprisings
and sacrifice
in multiples of silence
beyond the splints
and braces, to the
other side of dark
forests of alphabet
and print.

Zephyrs, at the top of my life

is a train
                whistling through the night
blue zephyrs in my mouth,
                    an ornament of tears
        a relief into which I plunge.

a sea,
                a eucalyptus ring
of aging broken sails,
                  a vineyard of perfect complexion
        and meridians compass south

a bell,
                a sudden burst of saffron
light in terracotta
                  cities of receding grace
        and tongues of saints and sinners.

a mandala
                rosewood beads of myrrh
soaked skin burning
                  fear sopped in a biscuit
        trade winds bearing no mercy.

a feather
                floating without a wing
a merry-go-round of smoke
                  a quotient in every bone
        and nowhere a multiplier.

ABOUT ANAND PRAHLAD

Prahlad is the author of two books of poems, *Hear My Story and Other Poems*, and *As Good As Mango*, several critical studies on African American folklore, and a memoir, *The Secret Life of A Black Aspie*. He is also a songwriter and musician, and teaches creative writing, folklore, disability studies and film at the University of Missouri, where he is the director of the Creative Writing Program.

ABOUT THE POEMS

These poems are taken from a manuscript in progress, that explores not only my own disabilities, including autism, cancer, and arthritis, but intersections of disability, blackness, and genderfluid identity in American society and within black communities. The poems' aesthetic is rooted in the languages of black music and in autistic sensibilities that include, for example, synesthesia and word meanings arising from their colors as much as from their conventional definitions. This clash between the conventional and idiosyncratic sense of words is at the heart of poems I am currently writing, and becomes a mechanism for pushing back against the historical silencing of the disabled and for creating expressions of a disabled reality, voice, and perspective. https://prahladauthor.com

DJ Savarese

Oberlin Diary

03/03/2012

Snow again, wind,
and brightly colored burkas
by *Northface*.

Spring is a lousy correspondent.

03/04/2012

Like the heart in its cage,
a college student in the library.

Blood pulses through the stacks.

03/05/2012

Waking up this morning, I smile.
Twenty-four brand-new hours are before me.
I vow to live fully each moment
And to look at all beings with eyes of compassion.

--Thich Nhat Hanh

03/06/2012

My birth mother lost six children
to the State.
Of the other five, I knew only my sister, Kelly.

Last night she friended me on Facebook.

03/07/2012

"Open a pop tart," says the toaster.
"Peel a clementine."

The past like a rabbit darts across the lawn--
it, too, is hungry.

03/08/2012

When I am terrified, I smell rancid meat;
when I am calm, fabric softener.
How can that be?

03/09/2012

Folding laundry, one can almost
believe in god—the soul
is an agitator
in which we bleach
ourselves.

03/10/2012

"Stop nodding off!" I say to the dictionary.
"Get to work!" I say to the reference books.

Midnight swims in an icy pond—
the fish at the bottom mouth hello.

03/11/2012

Before I had language, I understood
the word *comforter*. On the first night
in my adoptive parents' house,
the bed felt like a giant cotton ball—
the swab before the needle's prick.

03/12/2012

Except that there was no prick.
Accept that there was no prick.

03/13/2012

Maybe spring will send a postcard:

Having fun in Florida. Wish you were here!

03/14/2012

Waking up this morning, I smile...

Meditation, it must be said, is difficult—
my stomach meditates better than my lungs.

03/15/2012

I have twenty-six pairs of pants—
with enough legs I can outrun anything.

03/16/2012

Like seals squeezed onto an ice flow
the words of this textbook--
watch them waddle across the page.

03/17/2012

The doctor says that I am synesthetic:
I hear colors and see sounds.
My father's voice is a balsam fir.

03/18/2012

Going to the dentist is a bit
like having
the Department of Children and Families
come to your house.
What will they find?

03/19/2012

For me sleep is a luxury—
like fresh strawberries or espresso.

03/20/2012

How can one live fully in a library?
Learned cholesterol clogs the stacks.

Twenty-four lettered hours are before me.

03/21/2012

Today at the supermarket, I bought yogurt,
beer and razors for my father. His shaved
head resembles an observatory:
inside, it's always night.

03/22/2012

I must have anesthesia at the dentist—
it's enough to be trapped in a chair,
but to feel the gloved hand of the past
invade my mouth….

03/23/2012

Today we picked up my father at a rest stop on I-90;
his shiny, new Mazda had run out of gas.
The service station was closed.
How funny: my frantic father stuck
at a rest stop.

03/24/2012

In my first foster home they found bruises
cleverly hidden beneath my shirt and shorts.
Because I couldn't talk,
I couldn't tell them who had struck me.

03/25/2012

My father's father never bothered to hide his rage:
he'd just throw him against the radiator.
What my father remembers of that cold, cold man
was the sudden, shattering warmth.

03/26/2012

Did the daffodils oversleep?
The sun is scolding them.

Stupid sun, they drifted off while studying.

03/27/2012

How can one man be so sweet and nervous?
My father tells me to stop pacing,
but he can't stop biting his nails.
If heaven had fingers, they'd surely bleed.

03/28/2012

Because the mind is a farmer,
the mad cow of anxiety begs to be milked.
So out to the barn I go.

03/29/2012

When I first had anesthesia,
it took me an hour to wake up.
On the device that I use to communicate,
I typed, "Easy breathing forever."

03/30/2012

Like buds on the trees,
my friends in their dorm rooms.
The wind incites a party.

03/31/2012

Is the penis a wasp?
Does it have to sting?
The pretty ones play
in the hive.

04/01/2012

Waking up last night, I moaned.
The covers seemed to be a bandage,
and the light, an unfeeling nurse.

04/02/2012

Thich Nhat Han once wrote,
"Walk as if you are kissing the Earth
with your feet."

My feet drag like a ship's anchor.

04/03/2012

Time to hit the books.

When I grab my belt,
a hundred novels
begin to undress.

04/04/2012

Though the skin was meant for pain,
I want anger to be a footnote,
not the main argument.

04/05/2012

Thank god the Internet is distracting!
Thich Nhat Hanh:
"If you're going to struggle to read,
read things that are worth it."

04/06/2012

Like a drop of blood on snow,
a solitary cardinal.

04/07/2012

In fostercare I shared a room
with a sixteen-year-old boy
who had been sodomized
by his father—I was three.
At night he'd take his revenge, yelling,
"Get over here, Retard!"

04/08/2012

The Oberlin library
is a massive, concrete bunker—a testament
to endurance.
Think: Berlin, 1945.

04/09/2012

The Buddha said, "Your work is to discover your work
and then with all your heart
to give yourself to it."

A lawnboy, I spread words around like mulch.

04/10/2012

The peace accords of spring.
The tulips risk tomorrow.

04/11/2012

My father sends an email:
The survivor skills you needed then
are not the living skills you need now.
Give your lungs a rest.

04/12/2012

How can I fire the great welder Loss?
For twenty years he has worked for me.

04/13/2012

As metals fuse
through the application of heat,

so past and present
become one entity.

04/14/2012

Gainesville, FL.
Hornets circle the single-wide.
My birthmother, that drooping chrysanthemum,
wants money:
"Pollination will cost ya."

04/15/2012

Tax day for the taxidermist.
My hide hangs on the wall.

05/16/2012

The retard got an "A" on his term paper.
As at a baseball game,
the past applauds.

05/17/2012

Kelly, can you believe what happened to us?

05/18/2012

Once, my birthmother
rode past my adoptive parents' house
on her bike.

Or was it a pair of broken spectacles?
Those spinning orbs seemed
to squeal inside my head.

All beings…eyes…compassion.

ABOUT DJ SAVARESE

DJ Savarese is currently an Open Society Foundations Human Rights Initiative Youth Fellow. *Deej*, the documentary that he starred in, wrote, and coproduced, recently won a Peabody Award. His creative work has appeared, or will shortly appear, in *Bellingham Review, The Iowa Review, Seneca Review, Stone Canoe, Prospect, Wordgathering, Voices for Diversity and Social Justice: A Literary Education Anthology*, and *A Doorknob for the Eye* (Unrestricted Interest Press).

ABOUT THE POEM

I value striking imagery above all else. In "Oberlin Diary," I let images do the work of daily observation. They become a kind of haiku calendar. They move forward and circle back; they gently mock a linear expectation of thought and psychological progress.

Anxiety is my almanac: the farmer in my soul swears by it. The moon, always full, rises above the page, casting its shadowy light. What I plant doesn't need the sun, or does it?

Nathan Spoon

With a Bubble Around Your Head

from the eye   of a turtle shell
from the tongue   of a lodestone
    when a storm is   impending
from the past

                    when

the Merrillian ghost   of a tiny hand
pulls a plug on what you say   your life
has come to   insisting   you cannot
possibly   know what   you know

now your shoe has become a raft
and you are adrift on it   you who
keep echoing more than yourself
to yourself as you breathe   alien

Fragile Rocking Horse Circle

I will put my hand on   a folder.
I am hungry for   a ham and cheese sandwich.
Tomorrow is fading
like the edges of   a wing.

There   is no clear line. The wing is   there
until it isn't. Tomorrow is running over the memories
of yesterday.   I wish I could make it digital fodder.
Even when   I put my hand on a folder   I confess I can't.

I used to think there were greats who   were rough with language.
I thought Ben Jonson was rough. I   thought Geoffrey Hill was rough
too.
I used to not like hearing the word   grab.
As a child I stopped using it

and convinced my siblings   to avoid it
as well. One day we were   talking to a neighbor
who said it.   All three   of my brothers turned
toward me and said   He doesn't like that word.

After our visit to the International Market I mostly   remember
the huge selection of fish on actual ice. Probably   anybody
who hasn't dreamed of being on ice at least   once isn't   human.
Probably they belong to that fabled tuberous   clan from space

currently ruling the world. Probably all of us who are   human
need to claim control of the world. Let's make   this orb our own.
Even as tomorrow and yesterday are fading.   Even as the present
like a thousand identical moths is repeatedly   dislocating itself.

Dark in the Guest Chamber

extremities over viral space   pieces of
rhythmic invasion fluttering   through
then pushing as if through   a wolf wall

here are the teeth as proof there   where
it is posed to match your existing   upset as
both of us plant faces into that   hive one

of us deservingly so the other with   a face
covered in a sustenance delicate as   a bunch
of stones smoothed by years of   a flowing

so soft it is called defiant forever   and so
subjected to roots as well as the   freshly
budding branches it is bright   occultation

and blocking bad input with good   input
rubbing the end of an eraser until   calm
returns my body to an envelope   of joy

Seeking Windfall

you are my   outride in the moment
my   meandering through | neural
planks | covered   in video scales

you are the day of my   calm might
oyster knifing between   applicable
cutting and pasting | until   we turn

temporarily rude   greeting you with
backpacks   floundering off | tender
backs   as we roll into escape rooms

screaming hello   by drenching you
in an avalanching of   facts   about
cuttlefish the size   of quarters   or

the | photosynthetic   monogamy
found around the big pincers of big
lobsters a fact not lost   on monsters

The Owl of Minerva's Education

What if the blandeur is mystical?
if drivers of dead sea vans are out
as absurd as it sounds to kidnap

themselves? if all of us are amazing
more often than we are mediocre?
In my dream one friend was looking

adoringly at the musical performance
of another who doesn't perform
music in waking life. Thank goodness

for friends! Thank goodness for
smart phones and my own efforts to
capture such tender moments even

while sleeping. Thank goodness
whether either ever knows how much
I care for them though neither is

as close a friend as they are to
each other. New pants are healing
wounds acquired by a nation

still waiting to grow into the dreams
ghosts have fashioned for it. Something
about a thing we all hate hearing about

is making it more than what it is. Now
no matter what we wear we will look
cute forever. Now no matter how

much menial texting she does her
engineering degree equals loads of
fast money. She may never be rich but

no matter. It is shocking how deep
the butterfly effect goes. I mean lives
merge and make new lives out of it.

Tubers

over the phone her little voice was shaking as she
admitted a wolf had climbed the stairs and
entered through the backdoor after hearing
commotion she had caught a glimpse of fur and
ears and tail and teeth then she ran and locked
herself inside a bathroom before calling

questions about

what   the middle button of predictive text

will deliver us from   remains a source

of anxious perpetuality   like lace

on a slip hanging
too far   below
the hem of a dress
on a coldish rainy day

in April the child
is adorable though
the child is clearly
the result of prosaics

what if the above-mentioned wolf   is
the result of prosaics too? if the house
we dream of living in is not yet our house
this   is proof we are wielding too little

force or too much farce
                I like farce
                farce
                makes us face how we are not what he cracked us up
to be he who is a perpetual farce

the relationship of coffee to yoga pants is a farce
the way a conversation's words lie together implying
things they do not mean is a farce
I like touching the mane of a farce
as I ride it into a cloud of constructs used for
deconstructing smol emerging models

ABOUT NATHAN SPOON

Nathan Spoon is the author of *Doomsday Bunker* (Swan World, 2017). His publications include *Poetry*, *Mantis*, *Oxford Poetry*, and the anthology *What Have You Lost?* (HarperCollins). He is  Senior Editor of *X-Peri* and has read his poetry at the University of Pennsylvania, Vanderbilt University and the ALSCW Conference.

ABOUT THE POEMS

A collage always begins with a first piece, some image or fragment that is begging to be combined with other images and fragments. Once this is done… voilà! Poems that are language collages are no different. A word, a string of words, a phrase, a sentence springs to mind and calls out for company. Soon there is a crowd. As with any crowd, what emerges between its members is a spirit of some kind. That spirit is a product of the crowd that has been gathered.

I recently discovered a book called *The Art of the Clean Up: Life Made Neat and Tidy*. Page after page elicits laughter and intrigue, since the thing—whether it is a pine bough, a fruit salad or a bowl of alphabet soup—is often ruined in the act of making it neat and tidy. This book helped me understand that it is alright for me write poems without trying to correct the inclinations of my brain, which is a dyslexic, ADHD and autistic brain, by "cleaning up" my crowds of language as they gather in the shape of poems. It is alright for my poems to be as wonderfully untidy as I can make them, because the spirit of poetry is wild and permeated with the mysterious.

LOST HORSE PRESS
is pleased to announce the publication of

HABITATION

Collected Poems by

Sam Hamill

HABITATION collects the best poetry from a career spanning more than forty years by the distinguished Northwest poet-editor-translator, Sam Hamill. Drawn from fifteen volumes of celebrated poetry, whether in brief haiku-like poems or long-ranging narratives, HABITATION presents a lyrical voice that is unique in American poetry today. Jim Harrison has declared, "Hamill has reached the category of a National Treasure," and Hayden Carruth has written, "[His] poetry is no less than essential."

SAM HAMILL was born in 1943 and grew up on a Utah farm. He is Founding Editor of Copper Canyon Press and served as Editor there for thirty-two years. He taught in artist-in-residency programs in schools and prisons and worked with Domestic Violence programs. He directed the Port Townsend Writers Conference for nine years, and in 2003, founded Poets Against the War. He is the author of more than forty books, including celebrated translations from ancient Chinese, Japanese, Greek and Latin.

A Letter to Han Shan-tzu

I think of you often these days,
old master, when some people say
my poems aren't poems at all,
but merely occasions
of political provocation,

and of course they may be right.
Like you, late at night,
I scratch my songs on a wall
by firelight, and drink, and bow,
only to begin again, somehow.

—*Sam Hamill*

To order books from Lost Horse Press:

LOST HORSE PRESS
105 Lost Horse Lane
Sandpoint, ID 83864

Voice: 208.255.4410
Email: losthorsepress@mindspring.com
Web: www.losthorsepress.org

or contact our distributor:

UNIVERSITY OF WASHINGTON PRESS
PO Box 50096
Seattle, WA 98145-5096

Voice: 800.537.5487 or 410.516.6956
Fax: 410.516.6998
E-mail: hfscustserv@press.jhu.edu

HABITATION

Collected Poems

SAM HAMILL

POETRY · ISBN 978-0-9911465-5-0 · 6 x 9 · 624 PP
PUB DATE: Sept 2014 · $25 US · $30 Canada

No one—I mean no one ever—has done the momentous work of presenting poetry better than Sam Hamill. His poetry is no less than essential.

—*Hayden Carruth*

When future generations want to know the truth of these times, they will turn to the words of Sam Hamill. This poet is a visionary—the kind of visionary who rolls up his sleeves and gets to work. In his, 'Ars Poetica,' he writes: 'We go down to the sea and set sail/ for a world beyond war, / knowing we will never find it./ We are not heroes./ We sail The Justice and The Mercy/ because these boats need rowing.' In these poems of justice and mercy, with great clarity of thought and language, Sam Hamill defines a culture of conscience.

—*Martin Espada*

Sam Hamill has reached the category of a National Treasure though I doubt he'd like the idea.

—*Jim Harrison*

Sam Hamill is a writer unabashedly taking his place within the community of literature and the community of all sentient beings—his fidelity is to the magnificent truth of existence, and to its commensurate singing.

—*Jane Hirshfield*

The shape of Sam Hamill's mind is the shape of both a revolutionary and a monk at work. His sacred text is poetry.

—*Terry Tempest Williams*

**Perfect Crime by David Weiss is the newest book
from Nine Mile Books.**

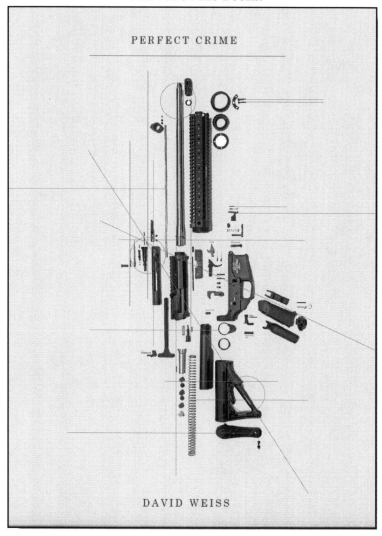

$16 at the Nine Mile website, ninemile.org, or Amazon at https://
www.amazon.com/Perfect-Crime-David-Weiss/dp/0997614765/
ref=sr_1_1_twi_per_1?
s=books&ie=UTF8&qid=1535452346&sr=1-1&keywords=perfect
+crime+david+weiss.

Readers write about *Perfect crime*:

Perfect Crime is a haunted book. In it one feels a pas de deux of despair and obliquity, of image and abstraction. A wry, humorous darkness broods over the pages. Greek myths that thread through the book--Demeter, Andromache, Chronos, Kore, Echo, Hermes and the gang--imply a larger pattern of doom for humans--humans who have "expiration dates" and are usually crushed in their passionate contacts with gods. In the face of such doom, the human exercise of consciousness, through language, is a brave defiance, that these poems act out in page after page. Perfect Crime feels like one long poem, a "highway / with no exit ramps" and "no exits," coherent in tone and method. — Rosanna Warren

Perfect Crime is brilliant! — Jody Stewart

It seems a perfect example of a poet and poems that make the ordinary extraordinary. And, of course, vice versa. And he does it all with evocative and shifting shades of loss. Also with humor. I was dipping into it and reading various poems, but now I like reading it straight through. I'm the lucky recipient of a very fine collection of poems. — Diana Pinckney

It's an indelible volume. I'm enjoying it greatly. — Diane Weiner

A new book by Nine Mile editor Stephen Kuusisto.

"That Stephen Kuusisto enables us to see the world through his blind eyes as well as through the 'seeing eyes' of his dog is this book's amazing, paradoxical achievement."

—BILLY COLLINS

HAVE DOG, WILL TRAVEL

A Poet's Journey

STEPHEN KUUSISTO

Praise for Have Dog Will Travel:

"Never before has the subtle relationship of a blind person to a guide dog been clarified in such an entertaining way. That Stephen Kuusisto enables us to see the world through his blind eyes as well as through the "seeing eyes" of his dog is this book's amazing, paradoxical achievement."
---Billy Collins

"A perceptive and beautifully crafted memoir of personal growth, and a fascinating example of what can happen when a person and a dog learn to partner with one another."
---Temple Grandin

It wasn't until the age of 38 that Stephen Kuusisto got his first guide-dog, Corky, and they embarked upon a heart-stopping and wondrous adventure. Kuusisto's lyrical prose gives his story a vivid quality, placing us directly into his shoes as his relationship with Corky changes him and his way of being in the world. Profound and deeply moving, this is the story of a spiritual journey: discovering that life with a guide dog is both a method and a state of mind.

Stephen Kuusisto is the author of the memoirs *Planet of the Blind* and *Eavesdropping: A Memoir of Blindness and Listening* and of the poetry collections *Only Bread, Only Light* and *Letters to Borges*. His website is www.stephenkuusisto.com.

The Golem Verses

poems by **Diane R. Wiener**

Buy it at the Nine Mile website, ninemile.org, or at Amazon at https://
www.amazon.com/Golem-Verses-Diane-Wiener/dp/099761479X/
ref=sr_1_1_twi_pap_2?

Praise for the new Nine Mile Book, The Golem Verses, by Diane R. Wiener:

Poet Diane Wiener unlocks the door to a room of confidences, secrets, passions, and fears. These poems present an interior dialogue in which the Golem is more than symbol or legend but trusted companion and guiding, grounding force. This room is furnished with intellect, wonder, inquiry, discovery, revelation, and release. Curl up in a comfy chair and bear witness to this lyric journey.
—Georgia A. Popoff, author of *Psalter: The Agnostic's Book of Common Curiosities*.

In Diane Wiener's original and fearless debut collection, we enter a dreamscape where Jewish mysticism, childhood games, pop culture and poetry's canon are blended together and all fair game. At its heart is Golem —part advisor, part imaginary playmate, possible lover—a mythical figure who "believe[s] she can be anything" and is playful, wise, and always kind. Wiener welcomes us into a magical, mystifying world that is somehow also intimate and familiar. "Tie the bows," she generously tells us, "hem your brushed brown trousers. Lean in, I'm here."
—Ona Gritz, author of the poetry collection, *Geode* and the memoir, *On the Whole: A Story of Mothering and Disability*.

I never knew a Golem until Diane introduced me. Diane's courage in embracing and welcoming the Golem allows us all to travel with them from "believing I was gone, remembering my own life" to "hindsight is rhubarb, associations strawberry preserved stick." What a glorious, wild, courageous adventure and a pleasure to read.
—Jackie Warren-Moore, poet, playwright, theatrical director, freelance writer. Her work has been published nationally and internationally.

Diane R. Wiener is an educator, social worker, advocate, singer, bassist, and artist. She has published widely on issues related to social justice, pedagogy, and empowerment. Diane is the full-time Director of the Syracuse University Disability Cultural Center, and she teaches part-time for the university's Renée Crown University Honors Program. *The Golem Verses* is her first full-length poetry collection.

A Little Gut Magic

poems by **Matthew Lippman**

Praise for the new Nine Mile Book, A Little Gut Magic, by Matthew Lippman:

I love this book. These are the most natural poems I've ever read. How they flow. How they touch the heads of thoughts so lightly and lovingly and move on. I say this is as someone who runs from even the rumor of a party: If these poems were people I would so crash their jamboree. "A Little Gut Magic" invents a genre: imaginative decency. Is that a genre or a style? Is this a book or an embrace? In these spikey days of distance and exclusion, Matthew Lippman is trying hard to find room for everyone, and almost succeeds. —Bob Hicok, author of most recently, *Hold*.

The world needs a poetry as loving and lyric, as engaged and ardent, as Matthew Lippman's is right now. Epitomized by deep connectedness and humanity, each poem reaches out to name our *happiness pain*, to comfort and stir us up, all at once. Generous and available, Lippman's poems establish an intimacy that feels easy, but is born of a hard-won wisdom, fueled by willful optimism. *A Little Gut Magic* is the real thing. Feel it. Trust it. It's a tome for our times. —Tina Cane, author of *Once More With Feeling*

Reading Matthew Lippman's poems feels like having a conversation with a hilarious, brutally honest, and brilliant friend." — Jessica Bacal, *Mistakes I Made at Work: 25 Influential Women Reflect on What They Got Out of Getting It Wrong.*

Matthew Lippman is the author of four poetry collections—*The New Year of Yellow* (winner of the Kathryn A. Morton Prize, Sarabande Books), *Monkey Bars, Salami Jew,* and *American Chew* (winner of the Burnside Review of Books Poetry Prize).